DECONSTRUCTING DOLLS

Deconstructing Dolls

Girlhoods and the Meanings of Play

Edited by
Miriam Forman-Brunell

berghahn
NEW YORK · OXFORD
www.berghahnbooks.com

Published in 2021 by
Berghahn Books
www.berghahnbooks.com

© 2021 Berghahn Books

Originally published as a special issue of *Girlhood Studies:*
Volume 5, issue 1 (2012)

Library of Congress Cataloging-in-Publication Data
Names: Forman-Brunell, Miriam, 1955– editor.
Title: Deconstructing dolls : girlhoods and the meanings of play / edited by
    Miriam Forman-Brunell.
Description: New York, N.Y. : Berghahn Books, 2021. | Includes
    bibliographical references.
Identifiers: LCCN 2020053968 | ISBN 9781800731028 (hardback) | ISBN
    9781800731035 (paperback) | ISBN 9781800731042 (ebook)
Subjects: LCSH: Dolls—Social aspects. | Play—Social aspects. | Girls. | Sex role
    in children
Classification: LCC GN455.D64 D44 2021 | DDC 688.7/221—dc23
LC record available at https://lccn.loc.gov/2020053968

British Library Cataloguing in Publication Data
A catalogue record for this book is available from the British Library

ISBN 978-1-80073-102-8 hardback
ISBN 978-1-80073-103-5 paperback
ISBN 978-1-80073-104-2 ebook

Contents

CʒꙄᴑ

Illustrations

ᗏᗌ

Preface

ℭℬℰ⅏

Deconstructing Dolls: Girlhoods and the Meanings of Play features the research of pioneering scholars whose ground-breaking work on dolls first appeared in a special issue of *Girlhood Studies: An Interdisciplinary Journal*. While serving as guest editor of the journal, I had been struck by the originality of the researchers whose imaginative studies clearly constituted a critical turn in a century of doll scholarship, especially robust since the 1990s. These GenX and Generation Y scholars expanded the focus and widened the range of approaches as they deconstructed dolls that remain fundamental to the construction of girlhoods today. These researchers analyzed the multi-layered realities embodied in Black, Jewish, handmade, paper dolls, among others, and mediated by contradictory ideologies, ideals, discourses and the perspectives of doll producers, consumers, and players. Their theoretically informed work provided new frameworks for the analysis of contending elements embodied in dolls, embedded in the cultures that produce and play with dolls, and encoded in historically-constructed categories of girlhood.

It was these investigations that served as an inspiration for *Dolls Studies: The Many Meanings of Girls' Toys and Play*, a scholarly collection I co-edited for Peter Lang in 2015. That anthology largely featured the work of other scholars similarly examining the making and upending of the racial, ethnic, national, religious, sexual, class, and gender ideologies and identities that constitute girlhoods. As for the trailblazing research that first appeared in *Girlhood Studies*, that remained less accessible to nearly everyone outside of journal subscribers and users. While every "special issue" of a journal aims to draw greater attention to a particular subject, the republication of the journal's original essays in this new book anthology is intended to achieve greater visibility through a wider distribution than the journal issue alone. Our hope is to acquaint a larger and broader audience of students and scholars, collectors and curators, and any one unfamiliar with the multi- and interdisciplinary field of dolls studies, with this significant scholarship—still on the cutting edge.

Acknowledgments

CREW

While studying the "new" women's history during my senior year at Sarah Lawrence College, I happened to come across previously unexamined documentary sources: a bevy of fashionably-dressed Victorian porcelain dolls. Differing considerably from the plastic dolls I had played with as a girl, the well-heeled, adult-looking China and bisque dolls seemed to be saying *something* about women and girls, though I knew not what. After spending the rest of the year trying to make sense of the research I had collected, I tried to shelve the project as I had the dolls of my own girlhood. But tried as I might to forget them, the dolls steadfastly refused to be cast aside. It was not long before I finally gave in, accepting that dolls—and girlhood—would not only be the focus of my dissertation but also sustain my profession as professor of history. Having just recently retired, the publication of this book is a deeply satisfying capstone to a career devoted to demonstrating why dolls, girls, and play matter.

I feel enormously grateful for the support I've received along the way and for this project in particular. I loved working with Claudia Mitchell, Jacqueline Reid-Walsh, and Ann Smith, who provided me with the opportunity to serve as guest editor of a special doll-themed issue of *Girlhood Studies: An Interdisciplinary Journal*. That experience introduced me to the original scholarship of an up-and-coming generation of dolls studies researchers from whom I learned much and to whom I remain indebted. I am so grateful to Amanda Horn, Associate Editor at Berghahn Press, for her patient persistence and confidence that the essays first published in the *Girlhood Journal* were well deserving of a wider audience. It has been my pleasure to work with Amanda and others at the press in order to remake this project into a book.

Over the course of my training and career, no one has been more steadfastly supportive than Claude Brunell, my partner in life and love for nearly 40 years now. His sweet devotion has sustained me day in and day out, to use a cliché that will surely make my mother cringe when she reads this. For it is my mother, Ruth Formanek, who I owe my greatest appreciation for modelling critically creative ways of seeing, thinking, writing, making and playing. Thank you, Doc.

Interrogating the Meanings of Dolls
Recent Innovations and New Directions in Doll Studies

Miriam Forman-Brunell

Custom80

Introduction

Understanding how dolls, as ubiquitous cultural forms, function in the lives of girls and in constructions of girlhoods is a scholarly endeavor that dates to the dawn of modernity in the U.S. In 1896, G. Stanley Hall, the founder of the child-study movement, a professor of psychology, and president of Clark University, co-authored, "A Study of Dolls." Informed by a recent appreciation of childhood and play but uninformed about changing notions of girlhood, "A Study of Dolls" narrowly concluded that doll play taught girls key lessons in femininity and maternity. Focusing more on race than gender more than forty year later, Mamie Phipps Clark, then a Master's student in psychology, utilized both Black and white dolls to study the effect of racial discrimination on the identities of African American children. The subsequent doll studies she conducted with her husband, Kenneth Clark, played a prominent role in the 1954 landmark desegregation decision, *Brown v. Board of Education*. Regardless of the insights of these trail-blazing studies, dolls' legitimacy as sources of documentary evidence remained mired in long-standing beliefs about the trivialization of girls and the devaluation of children's cultures. Further doll scholarship awaited the convergence of historical forces, theoretical frameworks, and disciplinary developments still decades in the making.

Nearly a century after G. Stanley Hall's "Study of Dolls," a new generation of scholars influenced by the emergence of girl-centered research, American Studies' interdisciplinarity, and the re-evaluation of mass culture by British cultural studies theorists, began to question the patriarchal imperative of dolls and the presumed passivity of girl players. New interpretive frameworks, historical contexts, and methods of analysis revealed that dolls were not uniform, static artifacts of a single dominant culture. *Made to Play House: Dolls and the Commercialization of American Girlhood, 1830–1930* (Formanek-Brunell: 1993), demonstrated that businessmen, women doll makers, and girls who were frequently at odds over the meanings of dolls, struggled to define the place and purpose of dolls in girls's lives and girlhoods. In addition to historians, dolls became the subject of scrutiny by psychologists, sociologists, educators and other academics all interested in what dolls had to say about girls' identities and grown-ups' ideals.

What accelerated doll research toward the end of the twentieth century was the rise of Girl Power, girls' studies, cultural studies, multiculturalism, the commercial success of the American Girl Doll (AGD) line, and the proliferation of the Barbie brand. Paying closer attention to the intersection of gender, age, race, class, and sexuality than previous researchers, Ann duCille (1994), Elizabeth Chin (1999), Mary Rogers (1998), Erica Rand (1994), Sherrie A. Inness (1998), and others in departments of English, anthropology, sociology, and Women's and Gender Studies examined Barbie dolls along with the beliefs and behaviors of doll players. While emphasizing the ways in which dolls reinforced normative notions and racial and gendered "otherness," their studies pointed to the ways in which dolls and the girls who play with them negotiate, revise, and disrupt the cultural categories of girlhood.

In the new millennium, scholars across the academy, cultural critics, and feminist activists continued to critically examine the role of mass-produced and mass-marketed dolls in the socialization, sexualization, commodification, exoticization, commercialization, racialization, and essentialization of girlhood. By the second decade of the twenty-first century, however, doll research pointed to new directions. Robin Bernstein devised an entirely new methodology for interrogating dolls in her path-breaking work, *Racial Innocence: Performing American Childhood from Slavery to Civil Rights* (2011) The scholarship first printed in the *Girlhood Studies* journal and republished here is novel for its use of a variety of critical practices in order to analyze the textuality of dolls and to interpret the embodied ambivalences, ambiguities and agency. Different understandings of dolls' meanings draw upon discursive backgrounds as well as overlapping interpretive frameworks: hip hop; Jewish history; fashion; and architecture, among others.

The varied meanings of dolls to different generations is readily apparent among the largely GenX and Generation Y (Millennials) scholars and their young research subjects whose viewpoints and voices are represented herein. Along with others, Janet Seow amplifies the embryonic critiques of girls "who do not yet have the vocabulary and skills to challenge the racial hierarchies of neoliberal consumption and playground racism." The contributors to this collection upend notions of scholarly objectivity by privileging subjectivities and professionalizing subcultural principles and practices—like DIY (Do-It-Yourself). Before discussing their research results, it is worth considering in some detail how the scholarly conversation about dolls is being furthered by researchers who intermingle disciplinary specializations; blend poststructuralist theoretical perspectives with feminist epistemologies and critical race theory; employ innovative sources of evidence; devise novel methodologies and research designs; revise what counts as a doll and who counts as a doll player, and consequently, explore new themes in doll studies—from cultural work to historical memory, reception practices to (sub)-cultural production, and the construction of identities (and buildings) to the functions of fandom.

New Disciplinary Approaches to Doll Research

The new approaches to the study of dolls have much to do with the training of these twenty-first century scholars. There are those schooled in literature with its deep roots in girlhood research and others who hail from communications which has generated the remarkable growth of cultural theory-informed girls' media studies. Doll researchers are also rising from more unexpected academic domains, such as architecture: one of the authors in this volume deconstructs Barbie's Dream House. The educational backgrounds of other doll scholars are even more multi-, inter-, and post-disciplinary. For example, cultural heritage studies incorporates elements of museum studies, cultural studies, memory studies, material culture, object studies, and anthropology. The relatively new field of book history that broadly examines the creation, dissemination, and reception of script and print, provides unprecedented opportunities to read paper doll publications in a new light. Combined, the changing academic landscape is complicating understandings of the artifacts of girlhood in ways that move beyond established approaches, dominant interpretations, and familiar critiques.

Theoretical Applications

Scholarly application of theories—from contemporary feminist to poststructuralist—is providing critical doll studies research with new frameworks for understanding how dolls and related texts like books about dolls function culturally, socially, politically, racially, and psychologically. Based on the understanding that narratives appear in a variety of literary and non-literary forms of expression, one contributor draws upon narrative theory in order to analyze the characters and stories in nineteenth-century paper doll books and to speculate on the meaning-making of children who read and played with them. In order to interrogate homemade dolls rather than store bought objects, another scholar turns to DIY theorist Henry Jenkins and his theory of "participatory culture."

Methodological Approaches

New doll scholarship is based on a variety of methodologies often creatively combined. Cross-disciplinary investigations link traditional methods (even ancient literary techniques like reverse chronology) with overlapping categories of analysis, and other scholarly methods including the more recent approach of off centering. By utilizing textuality—a methodological approach that examines the relationship between material culture and social meaning—memory work, and other methods, new light is shed on the dynamic gendered, racial, and socio-cultural meanings of dolls.

While one scholar utilized a participatory survey, others made creative use of ethnographic methods of research. April Mandrona devised an autoethnography. And the e-ethnography, an electronic method of doll data collection used by Molly Brookfield is characteristic of generational access to technology and ease with new media. The techno savvy of late twentieth-century girls' culture is clearly evident in the methods used by these young researchers. Data collection was made possible, for instance, by transforming a leading social media site into a research domain, using email, and blogs. In this study, and in Rebecca Hains' in which preteens videotaped their own doll play narratives, girls become active agents in the research process. At the same time, researchers like Hains and Brookfield who presented themselves as peers to those they studied diminished the divide between the girl subject and woman subject respectively, and the research scholar. To that end, April Mandrona interrogated her girlhood self: Annette Kuhn's (1995) memory work provided a method for analyzing personal items as historical objects.

Bodies of Evidence

These doll research scholars see dolls as dynamic texts that represent layered versions of realities that are mediated by often contradictory ideologies, values, or worldviews of doll creators, producers, consumers, and players. Consequently, their work engages the complexities and contending elements embedded in the cultures that produce and play with dolls and the conflicts embodied in dolls. "Placing the epitomes of girl culture and architectural culture, Barbie, and Modulor, in conversation,"

Frederika Eilers' "theoretical reflection probes the relationship between these idealized bodies, buildings, and typical users." Bodies function as critical sites whether the focus is on objects, images, or characters, dolls that are commercially-produced or home-made, paper or plastic, representations of girls who are Jewish, Latina, African-American, disabled or white. In addition to dolls' bodies, the authors consider those of girls and young women who use their bodies as doll players, producers, or performers. Collectively, the authors' investigations of multiple audiences demonstrate dolls' flexible (rather than fixed) meanings.

Just as the authors construct girlhood more broadly, they also have expanded understandings of what constitutes a doll and sites where they might be found. Fiction remains one of the most accessible documentary sources—especially so since the publication of American Girl Doll books. Yet, scholars like Hannah Field are also reexamining paper dolls, standing as they do at the intersection of material culture and print culture, mass produced and homemade creations. By examining the methods and analyzing the meanings of the goods girls make, investigators can mine a largely untapped source of information about girlhoods. Consequently, some of the doll-based research goes beyond childhood and even outside the proverbial nursery. Looking in less obvious locales has increased the variety of sources and sites of play and performance, and extended the study of dolls to include female adolescents and young women.

Doll Research Design

Despite the variety of methods and materials, the size and scope of the new doll research is often relatively small. Although not all, many of the studies are as diminuative as dolls. Janet Senow studied 10 girls and young women between the ages of 7 and 18 from Afro-Caribbean migrant communities in their homes in urban Toronto. Hains' study is based on an "afternoon's observation" of a handful of girls. During their "show-and-tell playtime," the girls made meanings that clearly diverged from the intentions of the dolls' producers and the interpretations of scholars. Molly Brookfield's study that provides insight into a generational cohort of doll players is based on scarcely more than a dozen research subjects. And then there is April Mandrona who examines one especially smallscale site of doll production—her own.

New Themes in Doll Studies

The methodological, theoretical, and evidentiary innovations currently employed in doll studies make possible the exploration of new themes, such as the cultural work of dolls and their role in the construction of historical memory. In her essay, Lisa Marcus examines the broader cultural purposes of iconic Jewish girls in the twentieth century. American Girl Doll, Rebecca Rubin, and the books bundled with her, extend and expand the cultural work of Anne Frank whose transformation into "Hollywood Anne" played an important role in the reconstruction of historical memory. While lauded for introducing millions of girls to American history, romanticized representations of girls create a past that is acceptable and affirming, but not authentic. How girls renegotiate the past in light of present circumstances is evident in Rebecca Hains' essay about the ways in which Bratz dolls' racial diversity provided African-American girls with "an avenue to explore race, racism, and U.S. history."

Frederika Eilers considers the significance of girls being able to modify the designs of the early folded cardboard Barbie Dream House before the plastic model, requiring adult assembly, turned Barbie into a homemaker with a refrigerator and a stove. Hains' study of how Black girls receive Bratz dolls exemplifies the exploration of reception practices and (sub)cultural production. Enabling the preteens to videotape their own doll play narratives provides a unique lens into youthful productions of meanings. Hains shows that the girls' appropriation of the dolls with various skin tones act out scenarios relevant to their everyday lives. Whether in the twenty-first century or the nineteenth, girls often play with dolls in ways that are contrary to commercial interests. Hannah Field finds that paper dolls show evidence of greater use than the commercially-printed books with which they were paired. April Mandrona's homemade creations reveal another way in which girls circumvent mainstream children's culture. She privileges the handmade artifacts of girlhood found in attics more so than in museums for the insights they provide into girls who also creatively construct dolls and girlhood identities.

Commercially-produced dolls are also sites of identity formation understood as shifting, performative, and prescriptive. The assimilationist identity of American Girl Doll, Rebecca Rubin, for example, draws upon a century of "fictions of Jewish American girlhood" similarly embodying broader cultural anxieties about difference and ideologies about belonging. The Fuller paper dolls designed to illustrate accompanying moral tales had surprisingly more mutable identities outside of their narrative context and content. Other authors show how the relational aspects of doll-related identities persist as girls grow into young women. How young women construct adult identities by building on girlhood memories is revealed by the first generation of American Girl Doll players. Molly Brookfield's self-presentation as an American Girl Doll "fan" is an identity she shared with her young adult research subjects. In her study, Janet Seow demonstrates the ways in which doll play with Black as well as white Barbies reinforced the racialized identities and marginalization of Afro-Caribbean girls in Toronto while at the same time providing opportunities to demonstrate their resistance to racial inequalities. Jennifer Whitney's study of Nicki Minaj demonstrates why her puckish reappropriation of Barbie's identity appeals to her fan base.

This collection begins with three essays that examine doll-and-book combinations from an intertextual perspective. Lisa Marcus's, "Dolling Up History: Fictions of Jewish American Girlhood," examines American Girl Doll Rebecca Rubin, and the box-set of books that accompany her. Marcus finds evidence of a repackaged "nostalgic and triumphalist narrative in which America figures as benevolent sanctuary and the Holocaust, American anti-Semitism, and the costs of assimilation are elided and smoothed away." Marcus traces the roots of this reassuring narrative to the Americanization of Anne Frank as a key icon of Jewish American girlhood. These and other "dolled up versions of history" stand in contrast to more conflicted ones by prominent Jewish women writers like the late Adrienne Rich, and serve as a caution against "buying into" nostalgic icons of girlhood.

Informed by the central assertion of book history that "forms affect meaning," Hannah Field investigates early nineteenth-century paper doll books in, "A Story, Exemplified in a Series of Figures: Paper Doll versus Moral Tale in the Nineteenth Century." Field examines the tension between the moral narratives in paper doll books that required female figures to undergo numerous costume changes (by actually changing their heads!) but subsequently degraded and disciplined the characters for their love of finery, fashion, and vanity. Did girl readers/players absorb the stories' textual morals or did they go so far as to read against the grain? The potential was certainly there as the book and the paper dolls could exist independently of each other. Field's analysis of the wear patterns of the paper dolls and their clothing suggests that girls' literary and play practices may have departed from the gendered expectations of publishers and parents.

Girls' responses to more modern morality tales are considered in "From American Girls into American Women: A Critique of Women's Nostalgic Readings of the American Girl Dolls." Molly Brookfield's study examines the complexities of nostalgia for American Girl dolls among nineteen young women who grew up in the 1980s and 1990s. Drawing upon postmodern theories of nostalgia and the meanings of objects, Brookfield challenges the persistent perception that girls are duped by dolls and that their nostalgia is naïve. Instead, she finds that reflective nostalgia among former AG doll players includes both affection for AG dolls as well as criticism of the company for commercializing and universalizing girlhood. Rather than romanticizing the past, the young women draw upon their ironic insights into their nostalgia in order to construct empowered identities attuned to the materialism of womanhood in the twenty-first century.

The second set of essays examines doll productions and performances beginning with "Barbie versus *Modulor*: Ideal Bodies, Buildings, and Typical Users." In this study, Frederika Eilers compares Barbie to *Modulor*, a figure devised by the modern architect Le Corbusier, in order to consider the impact of Barbie's unrealistic proportions on her Dream House. Eilers argues that when placing these objects in conversation with each other, the ideal body types and the model spaces designed for them share a common basis in modern methods and values such as the exclusion of "non-ideal" users like Becky, Barbie's wheelchair bound friend.

"Handmade Identities: Girls, Dolls and DIY" examines the study of dolls, girls' identities, and the contemporary DIY (do-it-yourself) craft movement, areas of inquiry that until now have remained separate. Departing from the more typical scholarly focus on mass-produced dolls and their impact on feminine socialization, April Mandrona uses memory work analysis in order to examine the doll-making activities of girls. She argues that young doll makers' creative productions are active negotiations of cultural meanings that make possible girls' participation in the construction of their girlhood identities.

Rebecca C. Hains' essay, "An Afternoon of Productive Play with Problematic Dolls: The Importance of Foregrounding Children's Voices in Research," expands current understandings of Bratz dolls by providing intriguing evidence of the dolls' oppositional potential among girls whose perspectives are often absent from scholarly studies and popular critiques. By making herself into a "near peer" and enabling girl subjects to record their collectively-produced stories with a camcorder, Hains provided favorable conditions that gave rise to unexpected results. While the girls in the study predictably marveled at the fashion dolls' "cool" clothing and accessories, they also disrupted the standardized fashion-based narrative that led them to identify as sexual objects. They did so by ignoring some prompts (such as the fashionable clothing) and responding to others: the Bratz' variable skin tones fostered the development of alternative scripts clearly not intended by the dolls' manufacturer. Like other *bricoleurs* who use DIY techniques (combining available materials into creative constructions), the girls' doll stories drew upon classroom lessons and mainstream media to enact their own historical understandings of racism, slavery, and freedom in the African American past.

Jennifer Dawn Whitney's "Some Assembly Required: Black Barbie and the Fabrication of Nicki Minaj" explores the public persona of hip hop artist Nicki Minaj whose controversial appropriation of the Barbie doll has generated both fandom and criticism. Using feminist and poststructuralist theory to understand the lyrical and visual performances, Whitney argues that Minaj's aim is to playfully subvert the iconic doll. In the process of co-opting Barbie, Whitney argues, Nicki Minaj provokes her fans to "liberate and pluralize how we think about Barbie, race and idealized femininity in the West."

Janet Seow's chapter, reprinted from a later issue of the *Girlhood Studies* journal, is informed by the qualitative research of Elizabeth Chin (1999) and Rebecca Hains (2012) that examined the effects of doll culture, race, representation, and consumption on the social world and agency of inner-city black girls. In "Black Girls and Dolls Navigating Race, Class, and Gender in Toronto," Seow examines how racist and classist representations of dolls impact Black girls who convey through their play an understanding of "positionality and self-identity in a biased world." She argues that Afro-Caribbean girls' play with Black Barbies and Bratz dolls shapes racialized identities and marginalization. But that's not all. Their doll play also demonstrates girls' agency in circumventing their exclusion from dominant Western notions of girlhood. With the dolls they repurpose and the narratives they enrich, the players revealed their ability to navigate the "barriers that reinforce racial inequalities and social hierarchies in girls' material culture in a multicultural Toronto." The girl players also subversively rejected dominant identities and social characteristics embodied and inscribed in dolls. And by becoming "discerning consumers of a doll culture coded with values of the dominant patriarchal white society, these Afro-Carribean girls were able to generate alternatives in a racially hierarchal space.

By historicizing, theorizing, contextualizing, and analyzing dolls of all sorts, the authors reveal the complex meanings of dolls to girls and grownups across time, space, cultures, and disciplines. By exploring the dynamics among representations and reception, productions and performances, genders and generations, races and rights, the essays forge new avenues in the interrogation of dolls as artifacts of culturally constructed and lived experiences of girls and young women.

References

Bernstein, Robin. 2011. Racial Innocence: Performing American Childhood from Slavery to Civil Rights. New York: NY University Press.

Chin, Elizabeth. 1999. "Ethnically Correct Dolls: Toying with the Race Industry." American Anthropologist 101, No. 2: 305–321.

Clark, Mamie Phipps. 1939. "The Development of Consciousness of Self in Negro Pre-School Children." MA thesis, Howard University.

duCille, Ann. 1994. "Dyes and Dolls: Multicultural Barbie and the Merchandising of Difference." differences 6, no.1: 46–68. Ellis, A. C. and G. Stanley Hall. 1896. "A Study of Dolls." Pedagogical Seminary 4: 129–175.

Formanek-Brunell, Miriam. 1993. Made to Play House: Dolls and the Commercialization of American Girlhood. 1830–1930. New Haven: Yale University Press.

Inness, Sherrie A. 1998. "'Anti-Barbies': The American Girls' Collection and Political Ideologies." Pp. 164–183 in Delinquents and Debutantes: Twentieth-Century American Girls' Cultures, ed. S. Inness. New York: New York University Press.

Jenkins, Henry, Ravi Puroshotma, Katherine Clinton, Margaret Weigel, and Alice J. Robison. 2005. "Confronting the Challenges of Participatory Culture: Media Education for the 21st Century," http://www.newmedialiteracies.org/files/working/NMLWhitePaper.pdf (accessed 6 April 2012).

Kuhn, Annette. 1995. Family Secrets: Acts of Memory and Imagination. London and New York: Verso Books.

Rand, Erica. 1995. Barbie's Queer Accessories. Durham, NC: Duke University Press.

Rogers, Mary F. 1998. Barbie Culture. Thousand Oaks: Sage Publications.

Chapter 1

Dolling Up History
Fictions of Jewish American Girlhood

Lisa Marcus

෴

Introduction

In spring 2009 the American Girl Company introduced Rebecca
Rubin, a new Jewish American Girl historical doll (see illustration 1.1).
Girls in Los Angeles lined up at 4 a.m. for her launch; New York families could coordinate their visit to meet the new doll with a tour of
the Lower East Side Tenement Museum. Rebecca Rubin's debut was
exuberantly welcomed by both the mainstream and Jewish press, with
The New York Times running a detailed story on 24 May 2009 about her
origins and the extensive research that went into creating her. (Apparently, choosing hair color alone took years—it's "mid-tone brown" with
"russet highlights"). The *Times* reporter subjected the doll to a vetting

Illustration 1.1 • Rebecca Rubin Doll and Book. Photo Courtesy of American Girl

by Abraham Foxman, of the Anti-Defamation League, who confirmed that "most of the time these things fall into stereotypes which border on the offensive" (a fact evidenced by Foxman's own collection of Polish wooden dolls, depicting Jewish businessmen counting coins). The Rebecca Rubin doll, he was surprised to find, is a "sensitive" representation of Jewish girlhood (Salkin 2009). Jewish cultural critic Daphne Merkin (2009) wrote in *Tablet Magazine* about "rush[ing] to order her, despite my advanced years," and Jewish mothers enthused on the American Girl website (2010) as they ordered dolls and accessories for Hanukkah. One lucky doll recipient gushed, "She is just like me with greenish eyes, brown, curly, shoulder length hair, being Jewish, and loving acting. She could be my twin! I love this doll!." Another wrote, "This is the best doll ever!!!! She is soooo cute!!! It is also cool that she is Jewish!!! That will be very educational for so many people!!!! She is beautiful!!!!!!" A father, signing in as "Papa Rosenbaum" raves, simply: "Mazel Tov AG!" Real American girls can buy Rebecca for $95. They can also buy a Hanukkah set complete with a shiny menorah made in China, a Sabbath set that includes challah and shabbos candles, a school lunch kit that comes with a plastic bagel and the score for "You're A Grand Old Flag" (along with the flag itself), and a pricey bedroom ensemble accompanied by two kittens. Rebecca and her many accessories and outfits can be had for the whopping sum of $901.95 before tax.

Anne Frank, American Girl

So what can a doll tell us about constructions of Jewish American girlhood? I want to contend that the eagerness and hunger with which girls—and their parents and grandparents—embraced Rebecca Rubin as an icon of Jewish American girlhood is significant, because the version of American history for sale in the Rebecca doll and the books that accompany her presents an idealized America in which anti-Semitism and anxieties about Jewish American identity are minimized and glossed over. One might counter, of course, that narratives for children quite appropriately offer gentler, more optimistic visions of history. And, indeed, the Rebecca Rubin books promote an affirmative vision of Jewish American identity that, as the website insists, offers a "girl-sized" view "of significant events that helped shape our country, and … bring history alive for millions of children" (American Girl 2010). Yet the history represented in this work of children's literature is instructive precisely because it illustrates—and taps into—patterns of ideological desire that resonate more broadly throughout the Jewish American imagination: the desire for fictions of a tolerant and welcoming America, and of a Jewish American identity that fits comfortably within it.

To appreciate the significance of the appearance of a Jewish American Girl in our current moment, the importing and Americanizing of the tragically iconic Jewish girl Anne Frank is instructive, for it reveals many of the same ideological pressures that shape the Rebecca Rubin version of American girlhood. Critics have ably outlined the troubling aspects of Anne Frank's reception in the United States. Cynthia Ozick (2000) has argued trenchantly that Anne Frank's story has "been bowdlerized, distorted, transmuted, traduced, reduced; it has been infantilized, Americanized, homogenized, sentimentalized; falsified, kitschified .... A deeply truth-telling work has been turned into an instrument of partial truth, surrogate truth, or anti-truth" (77–78). She cautions that the diary is not "to be taken as a Holocaust document," and worries that it has "contributed to the subversion of history" (78). Her quarrel is with the popular reduction of Anne into a sunny icon of hope most evident in the 1955 play and 1959 Hollywood film that rely too much on the optimistic spirit of Anne's oft-quoted statement (taken out of context from the diary) that "in spite of everything" she believes people are basically good at heart. This "Hollywood Anne," as Tim Cole (1999) has called her, is quintessentially hopeful; she "comforts us that people are still basically pretty decent, thus silencing any challenge that the Holocaust might make to our naïve optimism in human potential" (77). As Bruno Bettelheim (2000) insists, the immense popularity of an idealized Anne stems from audiences' desire for a history that acknowledges the horror of genocide only to release us from the burden of its legacy:

> Her seeming survival through her moving statement about the goodness of men releases us effectively of the need to cope with the problems Auschwitz presents. That is why we are so relieved by her statement. It explains why millions loved the play and movie, because while it confronts us with the fact that Auschwitz existed, it encourages us at the same time to ignore any of its implications. If all men are good at heart, there never really was an Auschwitz. (189)

Indeed, such audience desires directly shaped the construction of a "Hollywood Anne." As Ellen Feldman (2005) reports,

> our need for a happy Anne, despite her profoundly unhappy ending, runs so deep that when preview audiences saw the last scenes of the original cut of the movie, which showed Anne at Auschwitz, they scrawled outrage on their opinion cards. This was not the Anne they knew. (n.p.)

That scene was scrapped and replaced with the hopeful voiceover.

One of the reasons Anne Frank's narrative is so popular in the American imagination, these critics challenge, is that "Hollywood Anne" doesn't really die, at least not in front of us. Lawrence Langer (2000a), arguing that "upbeat endings seem to be *de rigueur* for the American imagination which traditionally buries its tragedies and lets them fester in the shadow of forgetfulness" (200), suggests that "one appeal of the diary is that it shelters both students and teachers from the worst, to say nothing of the unthinkable, making them feel they have encountered the Holocaust without being threatened by intolerable images" (Langer 2000b: 204). Martha Ravits (1997) adds, "It has served like Perseus's shield as a polished mirror in which a viewer can behold the face of atrocity without being paralyzed by it" (18).

At stake in such critiques are important issues about the uses to which historical memory (or amnesia) are put. The Americanization of Anne Frank feeds a desire for a flattering and exceptionalist American self-image—one of benevolence, innocence, and affirmation of diversity. Mark Anderson (2007) writes that while child narratives such as Anne Frank's "had the undeniable merit of winning the hearts of mainstream, non-Jewish audiences in the 1950s and 60s ... they also set the terms for an Americanization of Holocaust memory that privatized and sentimentalized the historical event [and] ... they also depoliticized and sacralized the Holocaust, filed off the rough edges of the Jewish protagonists, and sought reconciliation rather than confrontation with the gentile world" (19). I share his worry that too often Anne Frank's story is embraced as a vehicle for "teaching tolerance" and that this is frequently based on what he calls "no cost multiculturalism," which "provides the illusion of diversity without requiring that anything or anyone actually change" and "goes hand in hand with an almost complete lack of historical perspective" (17). Startling, then, is the fact reported by Francine Prose (2009) that while 50% of American schoolchildren had studied Anne Frank in a classroom assignment in 2004, 25% of American teenagers in another study could not correctly identify Hitler (253–254).

That Anne Frank continues to be symbolically important to Americans can be seen in the plan, as reported in the *New York Daily News,* 17 April 2009, to plant at Ground Zero, in commemoration of the 9/11 attacks, a sapling from the tree that Anne gazed at from her hidden attic in Amsterdam. If such Americanization of Anne Frank weren't troubling enough, her transformation into an American girl was almost completed in 2004 when a Long Island congressman petitioned for her honorary U.S. citizenship. Though the petition was not successful, Islip Town Council member Christopher Boykin regards "America as Anne Frank's natural home. Who better than this country to afford Anne Frank citizenship? It's been a place that has been safe for the Jews literally since day one" (Clyne 2004). While history proves otherwise, it is compelling that an elected official would hold to such a romantic view of Jewish American history. But that view is matched by many, including the American Girl Company.

History for Sale

Sue Fishkoff (2009), writing for *The Jerusalem Post,* asserts in her review of the Rebecca Rubin doll, "Jews love history, especially their own." She goes on to suggest that

> Jewish parents hip to the American Girl formula of nicely-made dolls and well-written books about the period of American history they represent, wanted a piece of their own people's story to give their daughters. "This is our history, right here in this doll," says author Meredith Jacobs of Rockville, Md., host of The Modern Jewish Mom on The Jewish Channel. (n.p.)

Another mother, writing in to the American Girl website (2010), gushes: "I love that when you buy an AG historical doll—you are also buying a bit of the past!" I want to think here about what it means to "buy a piece of the past," particularly a piece of Jewish American history that has been sanitized and reconstructed in frilly white pajamas with two pet kittens. All of the American Girl historical dolls are created with a boxed-set of six books that lay out the girl's story in a particular year (always ending in 4) in American history. The books are researched, and include historical appendices that add authenticity to the fictional tales offered within the covers. Rebecca Rubin's story is set in 1914, a shrewd choice that was evidently vetted with Focus Groups and historical research initiated by the American Girl marketing department. Setting the fictional Rebecca, who is nine years old in the stories, in 1914 strategically allows the American Girl Company to present an upbeat Jewish American history that highlights "assimilation, blending in and becoming American," as the senior vice president for marketing, Shawn Dennis reports in the *Times* article (Salkin 2009). 1914 is safely past the Triangle Shirtwaist Factory fire (1911), prior to the lynching of Leo Frank in Atlanta in 1915, and well in advance of the drastic restrictions of 1924 that effectively choked off immigration from Eastern Europe, as nativist legislators sought to control the racial and ethnic make-up of the United States, sometimes explicitly stating that their efforts would curb Jewish migration. It also falls before the implementation of quotas limiting Jewish enrollment at elite universities, and importantly, it allows for a pre-Holocaust Jewish America unscarred by the Nazi genocide.

Housed within the confines of this carefully selected historical moment, the Rebecca stories construct an idealized, triumphalist immigrant narrative of a welcoming America and a Jewish American girl whose potentially conflicting identities are happily fused and only minimally challenged. In the first book, the question of naming is easily resolved when cousin Moyshe Shereshevsky announces, "it's no more Moyshe Shereshevsky... I am Max Shepherd, if you please ... an American name for an American actor" (Dembar Greene 2009a :8). While "Bubbie" grumbles that "you don't change a name like a dirty shirt," (8) her old world view is swept aside as Max—seemingly with no effort—becomes a rich movie actor and contributes his first paycheck to help finance the passage for Rebecca's cousin's family to flee the Pogroms of Russia just in time to avoid conscription in the war. Indeed, the Historical Notes to the Rebecca series feature a poster (on display at Ellis Island), which contrasts the anti-Semitic old world to the welcoming new world (see illustration 1.2).

When the cousin's family arrives, in the second book in the series, Max and Rebecca serenade the new immigrants with a loud rendition of "You're a Grand Old Flag," emphasizing "free" and "brave" in the lines, "You're the land I love, the home of the *free* and the *brave* ..." (Dembar Greene 2009b: 5). Even Bubbie nods in time with the music while "Grandpa" (too assimilated, we assume, to be called Zadie) taps his foot. The thick patriotism of this narrative offers a syrupy version of easy assimilation highlighted when newly arrived cousin Ana is featured in a duet with Rebecca singing George M. Cohan's lyrics at a school assembly to celebrate the arrival of a new flag for display. In the auditorium, under the golden lettering of the "names of famous Americans: George Washington, Thomas Jefferson and Abraham Lincoln" (66), the two Jewish girls belt out their patriotic song, pledging allegiance to a

Illustration 1.2 • 1919 poster contrasting old world and American possibility. Photo courtesy of Library of Congress and the Statue of Liberty National Monument

welcoming America in which new immigrants quickly lose their accents, assimilate, and move out of the tenements and into the American dream. This matters to American Girl marketers, because in order to sell this "bit of history" to moms like those cited above, Rebecca can't live in a tenement like the one Lewis W. Hine photographed in 1910 (see illustration 1.3). Her bedroom set has to be cute enough for little girls to want to play house with (see illustration 1.4), and should include matching pajamas for doll and girl.

To be sure, these books chronicle Rebecca's struggles as well, but these are limited to anxieties that are easily resolved. She manifests just enough nascent feminism to appeal to contemporary mothers, evidenced best when she grumbles about the gender-segregated synagogue in which her brother is bar mitzvahed. Scolded for her kvetching, Rebecca is reminded by Bubbie that, "to be a good Jewish wife and mother … you must keep the house kosher and observe the Sabbath every week. The men will do the Torah reading" (Dembar Greene 2009c: 6). She later performs a daring Coney Island rescue of her cousin stuck on a broken ferris wheel, asserting her girl power without really challenging the patriarchal status quo.

Her chutzpah resurfaces in the final, and most politically radical, of the books when Rebecca becomes a veritable voice for the union

Illustration 1.3 • Lewis Wickes Hine, tenement rear bedroom, circa 1910. Photography Collection, Miriam and Ira D. Wallach Division of Art, Prints and Photographs, The New York Public Library, Astor, Lenox and Tilden Foundations

after her uncle and cousin strike to protest the miserable conditions of garment workers. As Rebecca declaims from a platform on Labor Day, 1914, American Girl offers a nod to Jewish labor history, but it's all in the service of (Jewish) Hollywood. Rebecca's speech, we're told, is

Illustration 1.4 • Rebecca Rubin bedroom collection (includes kittens, for $178). Photo Courtesy of American Girl

indicative of her acting talent; as Max heads West to the silver screen, Rebecca's family learns that she's already been an extra in a film and has diva aspirations. It's "all good" for this (Jewish) American girl, because the book box-set ends with Rebecca feeling "like she could do just about anything" (Dembar Greene 2009d: 70). Contemporary girls can help by buying her movie dress ($32) and costume chest (a cool $100). Her soapbox and union activist outfit are not for sale, but maybe girls can make it if they buy Rebecca's Fashion Studio ($17.95).

All Of A Kind

If Rebecca Rubin and her family offer wholesome fare for twenty-first-century girls and their families eager to connect with Jewish American history, these characters find themselves in good company with a family of fictional girls who were introduced to a welcoming public over half a century ago. The *All-Of-A-Kind Family* books, written by Sydney Taylor and first published in 1951, are compelling precursor texts in that they, too, look back to the Lower East Side of 1912 as a paradigmatic moment for Jewish Americans.[1] Hasia Diner (2000) has explored how "[t]he Lower East Side has become fixed in American Jewish memory as the site from which a singular story has been told," a story of origins and "founding myth" that "bears a striking resemblance to the Pilgrims' tale" (7). She notes that it

> has all the markings of an apocryphal tale: a people persecuted in the 'Old World' picked up their featherbeds, Sabbath candlesticks, and samovars and fled to Atlantic ports. They never looked back as they traveled in steerage across the ocean to a land of freedom, their landing welcomed by a massive statue grasping the beacon of liberty. (7)

While Diner is most interested in how the Lower East Side has been sacralized as a site of cultural memory, just as important as the geographic location is the time frame from which the originating tale springs. A generation after Jews began fleeing Eastern Europe en masse in 1880, just before World War I, and before the nativist immigration quotas imposed in 1924, the 1910s offer a powerful temporal locus for this "apocryphal" (Diner 2000: 7) origin myth. Unlike Jaqueline Dembar Greene, author of the American Girl Rebecca books, Taylor didn't need the likes of a marketing research team to locate the 1912 timeframe for her tale. (Nor, in 1951, could she have imagined "featherbeds, Sabbath candlesticks, and samovars" transformed into mementoes to accessorize your historical doll.) She turned back to her own childhood on the Lower East Side to provide fodder for bedtime stories for her daughter, Jo, an only child. As June Cummins explains (2003),

> she always claimed that she wrote the *All-Of-A-Kind Family* stories for her daughter Jo, who asked 'Mommy, why is it every time I read a book about children, it is always a Christian child? Why isn't there a book about a Jewish child?' ... Taylor attempted to capture the past and present it to her daughter and other readers as personal and ethnic history. (325 –326)

The *All-Of-A-Kind Family* books—still widely revered and read by Jewish families—offer what Diner (2000) terms "a hermetically sealed world of Jewishness and love," set in a Lower East Side where "families could be observant Jews and enthusiastic Americans at one and the same time" (65). As Diner writes, "on Taylor's Lower East Side, American patriotism cozily existed side by side with Jewish life, uncontested by conflicting demands" (65). This is particularly evident in a chapter on the Fourth of July. While Taylor is careful to alert readers to the patriotism of the neighborhood through the American flags that decorate the tenements, these flags are never presented as an oxymoron that puts into question the immigrants' loyalty or patriotism (as happens in the Rebecca book discussed above).[2] Taylor's books affirm Jewish Americanness as unproblematic and uncontested. For example, the family celebrates Independence Day with potato kugel and firecrackers, exhilarating in the "crusty brown" deliciousness of the kugel, and the sparkling firework display that follows. While the chapter affirms patriotic Americanness, it is tempered by a Jewish immigrant flavoring: "From tenement house windows and from storefronts flew American flags of all sizes" (1989: 135)

Cummins (2003) reports that Taylor's series, "read by Jews and non-Jews alike … lovingly describes Jewish rituals and holidays, simultaneously educating those readers unfamiliar with these traditions and affirming the experiences of children who know them already" (324). For Jewish readers, like Taylor's daughter Jo, the books "obviously validate Jewish observance and identity," as Cummins notes (324). This is best evidenced in the way that the narrative of the first book is structured around the seasonal calendar of Jewish holidays. The "lovely feeling of peace and contentment" that suffuses the Sabbath chapter allows Taylor to serve up Jewish tradition and ritual along with gefilte fish and chicken soup (1989: 78). Rather than overwhelming readers with didactic religious instruction, Taylor instead presents Jewish ritual as warm and inviting, almost as local color.

Accordingly, Taylor's narrative simultaneously functions to introduce Jews and Jewishness to a larger American audience unfamiliar with Jewish tradition and religious practice. The *All-Of-A-Kind* family seems carefully crafted to fulfill an intermediary or liminal role, bridging the Jewish and gentile worlds; they are "like" but "unlike" their Lower East Side neighbors, all-of-a-kind, but also all-American.[3] In the third chapter we move away from the domestic world of Mama and her girls, a world in which daily dusting is made into a clever game in order to instruct the daughters to be "the best little housekeepers in the whole world" (33), to the exterior landscape of the East Side, which "was not pretty." In a paragraph punctuated by negatives ("no grass"; "no flowers"; "no tall trees"; and "no running brook," readers are stripped of any pastoral illusions that might accompany the quaint domesticity, and are reminded of the urban landscape that "smelt of fish, ships and garbage" (34). We learn that "[l]ike many other families, Mama and Papa and their children lived in the crowded tenement house section of the Lower East Side of New York City. But unlike most of these families, their home was a four-room apartment which occupied an entire floor in a two-storied private house" (35). The family's difference from their "not pretty" surroundings is highlighted by their spotlessly clean home, and though all five girls share one bedroom, their "all-of-a-kind" difference from the rest of the community is subtly noted when they are shopping for the Sabbath:

> Only one tongue was spoken here—Yiddish. It was like a foreign land right in the midst of America. In this foreign land, it was Mama's children who were the foreigners since they alone conversed in an alien tongue—English. (72)

The girls' status as "like" but "unlike" their "foreign" neighbors makes them fitting guides for readers unfamiliar with this "foreign land right in the midst of America." Mama, too, proves a usefully liminal character in the figure she cuts:

> [T]he children were very proud of Mama. Most of the other Jewish women in the neighborhood had such bumpy shapes. Their bodies looked like mattresses tied about in the middle. But not Mama. She was tall and slim and held herself proudly. Her face was proud too. (65)

Mama's slender body, in contrast with her more lumpy peers aligns her with the gentile "Library Lady" (described earlier as "fresh and clean and crisp," slender, with light hair and clean nails) and marks her as a useful guide to help navigate readers through "the foreign land right in the midst of America."

That the all-of-a-kind family is positioned to make Lower East Side Jews accessible to a wider readership is evident in the way Taylor introduces gentile characters as surrogates for readers, and it is through these figures that many of the Jewish holidays are experienced. Because of their presence in key scenes, Taylor is able to offer a primer on Jewish Holidays (a kind of *Jewish Holidays 101*) without seeming to dumb down Judaism for the already initiated. More fundamentally, these surrogates serve to symbolize the relationship between Jews and gentiles, a relationship that in Taylor's depiction is both one of accessible and comfortable interaction, and yet one in which difference is maintained. Charlie, a beloved young peddler, "handsome, blond, and blue-eyed," and who, we later learn, has a WASP pedigree, a "wealthy family" and "fine education" (41), joins the family for many holiday gatherings, for "he was always at home in Mama's house, even when he was the only gentile present" (101). Taylor, through Charlie, makes a wide readership "at home" amongst her Jewish family, instructing readers in customs and traditions without becoming too anthropological. When daughter Ella sings "a mournful Jewish melody" (103) on Purim, Charlie's praise cements her crush on him. Yet, in a surprising plot twist, Charlie is revealed to be betrothed to none other than the girls' darling "Library Lady" (169), whom he rediscovers in the all-of-a-kind family's Succah. We learn that Charlie's family had opposed their marriage because his sweetheart had no family, that they had each (unbeknown to the other) fled to the Lower East Side, with Charlie shedding his name, career, and prospects in anger at his family. That both of these orphaned gentile figures find comfort among the all-of-a-kind family, and that they find each other during Succos in the temporary shelter erected by the Jewish family, allows Taylor to show that the benign Jewish family—while influencing and nourishing gentiles with whom it has contact—will remain intact and all-of-a-kind together in their "hermetically sealed" (Diner 2000: 65) world. The resolution of this romance plot affirms that Jews can be part of America while ethnic (and religious) differences are safely maintained. With Ella's crush dashed, and Charlie appropriately mated with one of his kind, Taylor ensures that the only challenge to the family's of-a-kind-ness is the addition of a baby boy (named Charlie, of course) to the all-girl family at the end of the book.

While Cummins (2003) has argued that Taylor employs "strategies of assimilation" and Americanization, even though they are "not dealt with frankly" and seem to occur "at subtextual levels and even extra-narratively" (326), it is still remarkable that Mama's quaint family never faces the kinds of conflicts around assimilation that so often shape immigrant narratives. As Diner (2000) notes,

[i]n at least this Jewish home of the Lower East Side, traditional practices, holidays and Sabbaths in particular, caused no one embarrassment.

> In no place did Mama, Papa, and the girls… suffer any personal in-conveniences in order to fulfill ritual practice, nor did the demands of acceptance into the American mainstream rub up against the inherited, cherished ways[.] (63)

Taylor's placid narrative, penned in the late 1940s and revised for publication in 1950 and republished in 1989, offers a romantic portrait absent of tension. Cummins (2003) notes a fascinating exchange between Taylor and her editor, Esther Meeks, who wrote to Taylor, "The family seems to live in a world of its own—the Lower East Side, not America. I have the feeling that these episodes were lived and wonder if this isolation really existed" (334). Cummins contextualizes the editor's worries that "particularly today… the family [needs to] show some signs of being American as well as Jewish" (334), by reminding us that as Taylor was writing, the Rosenberg trial was stirring up suspicion against Jews.

What is perhaps most striking about Taylor's placid narrative is its juxtaposition to the historical moment in which it was written. This period—as Americans came to grips with the Holocaust, Israel was founded, and the Rosenbergs were arrested—was rife with tension and anxiety. It was a period in which anti-Semitism remained pervasive, as has been freshly evidenced by a recently released questionnaire about attitudes toward Jews conducted by the U.S. military in 1947, which revealed a troubling anti-Semitism among the armed forces, with 86% of those surveyed agreeing that "there is nothing good about Jews" (ThinkProgress 2010). It is thus understandable why the quaintly benign version of Jewish American history that Taylor constructs would be so desirable from the vantage point of 1950—when Jews were, as Karen Brodkin (1998) has argued, "not quite white" (60). While the Rebecca Rubin books in one sense are more frankly assimilationist in their vision—think of cousin Moyshe Shereshevsky transformed into Max Shepherd heading off to Hollywood—in another sense what is most striking about these two narratives is their underlying similarity: the fact that, in 2010, fully sixty years after the publication of the first of Taylor's *All-Of-A-Kind* books appeared, there is still such an appetite for a nostalgic tale about the Lower East Side, circa 1910, a narrative in which America figures as benevolent sanctuary, a golden land where the conflict and persecution of the old country is answered by an embracing and relatively harmonized America.

History Lessons

In "In the Wake of Home" Adrienne Rich (1993) writes with unflinching clarity of the nostalgia that often shapes the stories we tell ourselves about the past. Her poem offers a tough-minded political critique of the seductive ideal of home while simultaneously expressing a compassionate appreciation for the human desire that craves it. Writing, knowingly,

> you will be drawn to places
> where generations lie
> side by side with each other:
> fathers, mothers and children
> in the family prayerbook
> or the country burying-ground

Rich acknowledges the longing for a coherent family history, a hope

> that once at least it was all in order
> and nobody came to grief (120)

Even as she articulates such desire, Rich portrays it as tied to romanticized ideas of a traditional past:

> You imagine an alley   a little kingdom
> Where the mother-tongue is spoken [...]
> a tenement where life is seized by the teeth [...]
> you imagine this used to be
> for everyone   everywhere (121 –122)

Rich insists on exposing the "hole torn and patched over" (121) in overly coherent narratives of the past that are seductive yet potentially dangerous in the way they romanticize history: "What if I told you your home / is this continent of the homeless / of children sold   taken by force," "—this continent of changed names and mixed-up blood," of "diasporas unrecorded," "underground railroads" and "trails of tears" (122). Rich suggests there is a freedom in getting beyond such romanticized ideals: "What if I tell you, you are not different / it's the family albums that lie," but then immediately she notes the imaginative and emotional hunger that persists despite or beyond such critical insights: "will any of this comfort you / and how should this comfort you?" (122).

The tensions that Rich locates in the pull of "home" illuminate the fictions of Jewish American girlhood I've explored here. On the one hand, it is quite understandable that the historical moment (circa 1912–1914) that both the Rebecca Rubin and *All-Of-A-Kind Family* narratives re-write exerts a seductive pull on Jewish Americans, for it anchors a kind of authenticating narrative that is both positive and exemplary—where Jews become the quintessential American immigrants embracing and embraced in return by the nation. Like many American Jews, I, too, can trace a family history to the narrative encapsulated in this paradigmatic moment. My grandmother came to the U.S. as a three-year-old in 1914—a Russian Jewish immigrant from Soroki, Moldova, a town whose name translates literally as "poverty." She traveled from Hamburg to Ellis Island in steerage on the last sailing of *The Pennsylvania* before the outbreak of World War I. Her name was Zlata Jampolski, the youngest child of Azreal and Shendel Jampolski, and their family of ten appear to have bypassed the Lower East Side and settled directly in Brooklyn. Captured in a Coney Island photograph from the mid 1920s (see illustration 1.5), my grandmother, in a revealing bathing suit, is leaning over her old-world father, clad in suit and tie.

The iconography of this photograph, with the bespectacled, patriarchal Azrael surrounded by his scantily clad daughters, fits right into a classic immigrant myth—highlighting the contrast between the older generation, still dressed in traditional garb and ways, and their Americanized offspring. By 1930, my grandmother had shed her identity as Zlata Jampolski, registering her name as "Jean Jay." Within several years she would be married, would give birth to my father (who would go on to obtain an Ivy League education), would secure a foothold in the American dream. I am almost certain my grandmother would have endorsed this optimistic take on her life story; accordingly, I have little doubt that she would have celebrated the assimilationist, quintessentially American Rebecca Rubin, joining in spirit her peers on the American Girl website cheering the arrival of this new version of American Girl(hood).

On the other hand, like Rich, I am also cognizant of the dangers of histories that idealize the past. Even the story I've told about my grandmother—culled, as Rich depicts, from "old family albums / with their smiles"—leaves out, among other things, the "subtle but powerful" (Karabel 2005: 303) anti-Semitism of Princeton in the 1950s, doc-

Illustration 1.5 • Azreal Jampclski at Coney Island with author's grandmother (private collection)

umented by Jerome Karabel ard experienced by my father. Just because I can tie my grandmother to what Hasia Diner (2000) calls the "apocryphal tale" (7) of Jewish American origins, to the moment offered by American Girl Company as the touchstone of Jewish American history, doesn't mean that I must offer it as a tale in which "nobody came to grief" (Rich 1993: 120), for as Rich reminds us, sometimes "it's the family albums that lie" (122).

Narratives that stress immigrant assimilation and belonging not only promote an exceptionalist vision of America as benign, tolerant, and just; in their erasure of conflict, oppression, and resistance, they also fail to offer models for confronting injustice in a complex world. Elizabeth Marshall (2008/2009), writing of American Girl's Latina *Josefina* doll, argues that "the creators at American Girl favor a white-washed … history" in which "issues such as racism, colonization, and war" are "presented as things that America has overcome," and that "avoids any lessons about social activism … to fight ongoing gender and/or racial discrimination" (n.p.) When I first presented a version of this piece (at a Holocaust conference), a historian colleague of mine provocatively advocated for historical amnesia, arguing that children need narratives that stress harmony and tolerance not ones that per-petuate conflict and division. Overlooking the chutzpah of invoking historical amnesia at a Holocaust conference, I would insist that chil-dren are ill-served by sanitized and overly cheerful fictional histories. As Sherrie Inness (1998) notes, "[p]eople often wish to view children's literature and children's culture as politically and ideologically neutral and naïve" (170), yet the ideological tensions at play in the children's texts discussed above clearly suggest otherwise. Historian Lisa Gordon, interviewed by Stephen Kinzer for the *New York Times,* 6 November 2003, about the American Girl series, critiques

> the 'obvious dumbing-down' of complex topics. … It's a mistake to think that children don't like scary or painful things. … If you think about fairy tales, they are often extremely scary or violent, and children love them for precisely that reason. (n.p.)

Adrienne Rich provides a striking account of the "belated rage" that can emerge when young people who've been denied access to darker histo-ries are confronted with them. In her essay "Split at the Root: an Essay on Jewish Identity," Rich (1986) chronicles a memory from 1946—of being sixteen and viewing alone a newsreel of the Allied liberation of concentration camps. She laments that she had "nobody in my world with whom I could discuss those films," that she "had no language for anti-Semitism," no ability to even ask "are those men and women 'them' or 'us'?" (107).

I am not advocating stories that dogmatically emphasize oppres-sion and victimhood. American Girl has already ventured into that territory in its construction of the African-American doll Addy (whose story begins in slavery), participating in the overwhelming tendency in American popular culture to portray African-Americans as perpetual victims, pathologically impoverished, forever linked to slavery and its aftermath. Yet, as Jeanne Brady (1994) has argued, the "chocolate cake with Vitamins" approach to history peddled by American Girl, in which "history and politics are disguised in the image of nostalgia, innocence, and simplicity," deprives girls of the "opportunity to read and understand history in all its complex forms in order to help them problematize the past and begin to see themselves as historical beings who can challenge the present and create a more democratic future" (5). The benefit of more historically complex fictions is not simply to teach children to see oppression in the past, but rather to acknowledge the structures of inequality and prejudice that call us to solidarity with others in the present. Narratives of Jewish American girlhood that more forthrightly acknowledge anti-Semitism not only prepare young readers for a world in which the anti-Semitism prevalent in the 1920s and 1950s has not simply vanished, but equip them to understand contemporary iterations of nativist prejudices, such as those undergirding recent immigration legislation.

In *The Holocaust in American Life,* Peter Novick (1999) concludes,

> Along with most historians, I'm skeptical about the so-called lessons of history. I'm especially skeptical about the sort of pithy lessons that fit on a bumper sticker. … If there are lessons to be extracted from encountering the past, that encounter has to be with the past in all its messiness; they're not likely to come from an encounter with a past that's been shaped and shaded so that inspiring lessons will emerge. (261)

Jewish American girls—*all* girls—deserve a more complex history lesson, one that hasn't been simplified to bumper sticker slogans that can be purchased on a website or in a megastore. There may be reasons to celebrate this doll that's not Barbie, that has chutzpah and performs tikkun olam,[4] but while the American Girl Company sold itself to Mattel some years back, we shouldn't sell ourselves short. Whether it's the problematic repackaging of Anne Frank's Holocaust experience, or the seemingly benign narrative of American Girl Rebecca Rubin, or even the beloved All-Of-A-Kind family, we should be wary of the icons of Jewish American girlhood we buy into.

Cʒ

Lisa Marcus is Professor of English and Chair of the Holocaust and Geno-cide Studies Program at Pacific Lutheran University. Over the last year she has been partnering with Seattle Holocaust Center for Humanity in teach-ing secondary school teachers to address U.S. racism and white supremacy in the Holocaust curriculum, leading book discussions, and lecturing about LGBT Holocaust history in Paula Vogel's play *Indecent*. Her recent publica-tions include essays on Holocaust survivor and poet Irena Klepfisz, immi-grant Jewish-American writer Anzia Yezierska, and a poem "I did not lose my father at Auschwitz," based on a trip she took with her father to Poland and Moldova.

ʒ

Acknowledgments

I dedicate this article to my late grandmother, Jean Jay (born Zlata Jampolski). Special thanks to Jim Albrecht, Miriam Forman-Brunell, Ann Smith, and George Tselos for help in bringing this article to publication.

Notes

1. Jacqueline Dembar Greene, commissioned author of the American Girl *Rebecca* books, claims that, "she didn't read Sydney Taylor's once-popular book series." Instead, she "re-read *Rebecca of Sunnybrook Farm* so that my character, Rebecca, might relate to the spunky character in that book, which was quite popular in 1914" (2010, e-mail to author).

2. In the scene where Rebecca and Ana sing "You're a Grand Old Flag," Rebecca worries whether Ana, who barely speaks English, is American enough to be authen-tically patriotic. Ana herself questions her loyalty to an America that has detained her lame brother Josef at Ellis Island. True to the optimistic formula of the series, the book ends with Josef's release and Ana "feeling *patriotic*" (Dembar Greene 2009b: 31–33, 70).

3. While "All-of-a-kind" refers to this family of daughters, the moniker clearly signifies much more, as my interpretation of Taylor's narrative suggests.

4. Tikkun olam translates from the Hebrew as "repairing the world," and usually calls for community service or activism.

References

"American Girl® Dolls: Rebecca Doll & Book." 2010. *Dolls, Books, Clothing, Furni-ture, Gifts for Girls American Girl®*. http://store.americangirl.com/agshop/static/rebeccadoll.jsp (accessed 16 July 2010).

Anderson, Mark. 2007. "The Child Victim as Witness to the Holocaust: An American Story?" *Jewish Social Studies: History, Culture, Society* 14, (Fall): 1–22.

Bettelheim, Bruno. 2000. "The Ignored Lesson of Anne Frank." Pp. 185–191 in *Anne Frank: Reflections on Her Life and Legacy,* eds. Hyman Aaron Enzer and Sandra Solotaroff Enzer. Urbana: University of Illinois Press.

Brady, Jeanne. 1994. "Reading the American Dream: The History of the American Girl Collection." *Teaching and Learning Literature* (Sept./Oct.): 2–6.

Brodkin, Karen. 1998. *How Jews Became White Folks.* New Brunswick: Rutgers University Press.

Clyne, Meghan. 2004. "Anne Frank, an American Citizen? A New Yorker's Quest to Make it So." *New York Sun,* 31 December.

Cole, Tim. 1999. *Selling the Holocaust: From Auschwitz to Schindler, How History is Bought, Packaged and Sold.* New York: Routledge.

Cummins, June. 2003. "Becoming an 'All-Of-A-Kind' American: Sydney Taylor and Strategies of Assimilation." *The Lion and the Unicorn* 27, no. 3: 324–343.

Dembar Greene, Jacqueline. 2009a. *Meet Rebecca.* Middleton, WI: American Girl Publishing.

Dembar Greene, Jacqueline. 2009b. *Rebecca and Ana.* Middleton, WI: American Girl Publishing.

Dembar Greene, Jacqueline. 2009c. *Rebecca to the Rescue.* Middleton, WI: American Girl Publishing.

Dembar Greene, Jacqueline. 2009d. *Changes for Rebecca.* Middleton, WI: American Girl Publishing.

Dembar Greene, Jacqueline. 2010. E-mail to author. 28 June.

Diner, Hasia. 2000. *Lower East Side Memories: A Jewish Place in America.* Princeton: Princeton University Press.

Feldman, Ellen. 2005. "Anne Frank in America." *American Heritage.com.* Feb.–Mar. http://www.americanheritage.com/content/anne-frank-america. (accessed 3 March 2010).

Fishkoff, Sue. 2009. "The New American Girl Doll: She's Jewish and She's Poor." *Jerusalem Post,* 25 May.

Inness, Sherrie. 1998. "'Anti-Barbies': The American Girls' Collection and Political Ideologies." Pp. 164–183 in *Delinquents and Debutantes: Twentieth-Century American Girls' Cultures,* ed. Sherrie Inness. New York: NYU Press.

Karabel, Jerome. 2005. *The Chosen: The Hidden History of Admission and Exclusion at Harvard, Yale, and Princeton.* Boston: Houghton Mifflin.

Kinzer, Stephen. 2003. "Dolls as Role Models, Neither Barbie nor Britney." *New York Times.* 6 November.

Langer, Lawrence. 2000a. "The Americanization of the Holocaust on Stage and Screen." Pp. 198–202 in *Anne Frank: Reflections on Her Life and Legacy,* eds. Hyman Aaron Enzer and Sandra Solotaroff-Enzer. Urbana: University of Illinois Press.

Langer, Lawrence. 2000b. "The Uses—and Misuses—of a Young Girl's Diary: 'If Anne Frank Could Return from among the Murdered She Would Be Appalled."

33

Pp. 203–205 in *Anne Frank: Reflections on Her Life and Legacy,* eds. Hyman Aaron Enzer and Sandra Solotaroff-Enzer. Urbana: University of Illinois Press.

Marshall, Elizabeth. 2008/2009. "Marketing American Girlhood." *Rethinking Schools Online* 23.2. http://www.rethinkingschools.org. (accessed 6 January 2010).

Merkin, Daphne. 2009. "Dolled Up" *Tablet*, 16 December. http://www.tabletmag .com/life-and-religion/22439/dolled-up. (accessed 10 March 2010).

Novick, Peter. 1999. *The Holocaust in American Life.* Boston: Houghton Mifflin.

Ozick, Cynthia. 2000. "Who Owns Anne Frank?" Pp. 74–102 in *Quarrel and Quandary.* New York: Knopf.

Prose, Francine. 2009. *Anne Frank: the Book, the Life, the Afterlife.* New York: Harper Collins.

Ravits, Martha. 1997. "To Work in the World: Anne Frank and American Literary History." *Women's Studies* 27: 1–30.

Rich, Adrienne. 1993. "In the Wake of Home." Pp. 119–123 in *Adrienne Rich's Poetry and Prose,* eds. Barbara Charlesworth Gelpi and Albert Gelpi. New York: Norton.

Rich, Adrienne. 1986. "Split at the Root: An Essay on Jewish Identity." Pp. 100–123 in *Blood, Bread and Poetry: Selected Prose 1979–1985,* New York: Norton.

"Rooted Remembrances: Tree that Gave Hope to Anne Frank to Blossom Wonderfully in U.S." 2009. *New York Daily News,* 17 April.

Salkin, Allen. 2009. "American Girl's Journey to the Lower East Side." *New York Times,* 24 May.

Sweeney, Meghan M. 2005. "Checking Out America: Libraries as Agents of Acculturation in Three Mid-Century Girls' Books." *Children's Literature* 33: 41–67.

Taylor, Sydney. 1989. *All-Of-A-Kind Family.* Follet, 1951. Reprint, New York: Yearling.

ThinkProgress. 2010. "Records Show Military Surveyed Troops' Attitudes Toward Jews in 1940s." 22 July. http://thinkprogress.org/justice/2010/07/22/176892/ exclusive-records-show-military-surveyed-troops-attitudes-towards-jews-in -1940s. (accessed 5 August 2010).

Chapter 2

"A Story, Exemplified in a Series of Figures"

Paper Doll versus Moral Tale in the Nineteenth Century

Hannah Field

ೞ

Introduction

In the first decades of the nineteenth century, Samuel and Joseph Fuller, London publishers and printsellers, produced a number of paper doll books for children. The formal components of these innovative early movable books, sold at the Temple of Fancy, the Fullers' pleasingly named shop on Rathbone Place, were consistent. Each set, packaged in a small sheath, was comprised of a black-and-white storybook containing the moral history of a young person (often in verse), a number of hand-colored cut-out images printed separately on card, showing costumes, and a single hand-colored cardboard head (see illustration 2.1).[1]

Illustration 2.1 • *Ellen, or, The Naughty Girl Reclaimed: A Story, Exemplified in a Series of Figures* (1811). The Bodleian Library, University of Oxford (2012), Opie E 34.

In most examples separate hats, slit so as to fit onto the head, were also included. While the Temple, which opened in 1809, is best known today as an historical artist supply business, these paper doll books were such a vital part of the store's trade that promotional material on the sheath to 1814's paper doll *Cinderella, or, The Little Glass Slipper* describes the Fuller firm as "WHERE ARE ALSO PUBLISHED Those esteemed and much admired JUVENILE BOOKS, with Figures that dress and undress"—the paper doll book becoming a metonym for the business as a whole.

The phrase "Figures that dress and undress," however neat and appealing as a marketing formula, elides the most noteworthy aspect of the format. The company might more aptly have referred to dresses which are headed and beheaded, since the clothes wear the heads, rather than the other way round: each costume has a small tab at its back, into which the stem of the head can be inserted to produce a complete paper doll figure that acts as a stand-alone illustration to the accompanying story. When I refer to a paper doll throughout this article, I designate the complete figure produced from the insertion of the head into the costumed body. The narratives of the Fuller paper doll books are not insensible to this quirk of the medium: *Ellen, or, The Naughty Girl Re-*

claimed (1811) counsels that, "[T]hough her face is fair and mild," Ellen is an extremely naughty girl (6): the discrepancy between Ellen's expressionless multi-purpose head, which cannot change between scenes as the costumes do, and the events at hand is registered in a knowing joke about the doll's form. (See illustration 2.1.) *Ellen's* full title is *Ellen, or, The Naughty Girl Reclaimed: A Story, Exemplified in a Series of Figures,* with the book introduced v_a the synergy between Ellen's story and the "figures" or dolls which straightforwardly exemplify it. However, in the Fuller paper doll books, the pleasures afforded by the paper dolls themselves undercut the didactic narratives or moral tales usually presented in the accompanying storybooks, just as a sly joke about the doll's format weakens any approbation of Ellen's naughtiness in the preceding example. This is especially relevant because of what I shall call the gendered morals in these books, which imply that female characters are more in need of particular moral lessons than are male characters.

Nineteenth-century Doll Culture and the Fuller Paper Doll Books

Historians of the children's book typically describe the success of the Fuller paper doll books as at once partial and short-lived. D. N. Shury of Berwick Street, Soho, printed the paper doll books for the Fullers, and they were released largely between 1805 and 1815 (Darton 1999), a period spanning the epoch of the Temple of Fancy's opening. Examples held in the Opie Collection of Children's Literature at the Bodleian Library, Oxford, which form a representative corpus, show a spike in production in 1811 and 1812, though the Fullers publish at least one title in the years 1810 to 1814. Peter Haining (1979) asserts that by 1817 the format had "fallen from favour in Britain" (15). The Fullers, says Percy Muir (1954), showed "less preoccupation with cost than with elegance of presentation" in their production of the paper doll books, leading to a high price for the works and in turn a rapid decline in popularity; he dubs the whole experiment "a comparative failure" (211–212). Although the format's hey-day was indeed relatively short, editions of Fuller titles appear until at least 1830, the date of the last example held in the Opie collection, an eleventh edition of Dr. Walcot's *The History and Adventures of Little Henry,* a title originally published in

1810. Moreover, only five years earlier (eight years after the supposed discarding of the format, according to Haining) an imitation entitled *Kathleen, the Irish Child* (1825) was self-published by one F. E. A. Staffurth, indicating at least some continued interest in the form. (The only known copy of this work is held in the Opie Collection.)

What place do the Fuller paper doll books have in doll culture of the period? The answer to this question can, in part, be found in wider accounts of the paper doll. Antonia Fraser's (1963) report of the paper doll's genesis forms part of her chronicle of fashion dolls, Pandoras, and pedlar dolls throughout the ages:

> It was the English who invented in 1790 a new type of Fashion doll, whose popularity was to last right through the nineteenth century, and is still in demand as a plaything for little girls. This was the flat card or stiffened paper doll figure, onto which could be attached a series of different dresses. At first they were made about eight inches high, and sold around three shillings. (43)

Despite the singular difference in the dolls' format (the full figure Fraser describes versus the tabbed head and slotted costume employed by the Fullers), the editors of this journal explicitly link the Temple of Fancy books to these late eighteenth-century paper dolls (Mitchell and Reid-Walsh 2002: 177). So, too, do Brian Alderson and Felix de Marez Oyens (2006). Fraser's (1966) broader account of the paper doll's purpose is unambiguous: the toy combines "the function of a doll with that of a fashion display in a more mobile and economical way than the earlier life-sized fashion dolls" (92) from which it evolved.

We find paradigmatic trends in children's clothes from the period in the Temple of Fancy paper doll books, suggesting that Fraser's (1966) assessment of the paper doll as "fashion display" (92) does apply here. Take Fanny's first costume from *The History of Little Fanny* (1810). (See illustration 2.2).

Fanny's combination of white dress and colored sash was typical of genteel girls' wear of the early nineteenth century (Buck 1996). The doll Fanny holds both mirrors and inverts her attire, sporting a yellow dress with a blue sash. Fanny's colored (as opposed to black) shoes and white (as opposed to colored) stockings reflect trends in children's fashion that Anne Buck (1996) traces to the first years of the 1800s, while the pantalettes she wears beneath her dress are perhaps more fashion-forward: Noreen Marshall (2008) isolates the period 1810 to 1850 as the peak of this garment's popularity. Some of the Fuller paper dolls locate each costumed figure in a *mise en scène,* but Fanny's only field of reference when she first appears is the square of red and green carpet, with a flower and trellis pattern, on which she stands. Her habiliments are the exclusive focus of the image; the clothes she wears are spotlighted and showcased.

While late eighteenth-century paper dolls and the Fuller examples share a number of features, the importance of one difference between the two products cannot be overstated—the Fullers' packaging of paper doll and storybook together and hence the paper doll's status as an illustration to a narrative. These books intimate a costume focus parallel to that of the dolls on their very covers: a full title like *Lucinda, the Orphan, or, The Costumes: A Tale: Exhibited in a Series of Dresses* (1812) multiplies subtitles, alternate titles, and colons in a textual equation in which the costumes the protagonist wears are as important as her situation, and the particulars of the story break down into "a series of dresses." Note also *Cinderella* wherein the preservation of Perrault's 1729 alternate title *The Little Glass Slipper* (in the original French "la petite pantoufle de verre") signals the importance of costume before the narrative begins. However, the texts of the paper doll books are moral

Illustration 2.2 • First costume from *The History of Little Fanny: Exemplified in a Series of Figures* (1810). The Bodleian Library, University of Oxford (2012), Opie E 55.

tales that inveigh against just the obsession with clothing that the paper dolls encourage.

Writing against a Love of Finery and Fashion

The status of the fashion doll, of which the paper doll is one type, as trend-carrier and promotional commodity was not unproblematic for commentators roughly contemporary with the Fullers. The Edgeworths ([1798] 2009), for example, in a famous critique from *Practical Education,* praise the doll as a "means of inspiring girls with a taste for neatness in dress" but caution that "a watchful eye should be kept upon the child, to mark the first symptoms of a love of finery and fashion" (11). Note that the Edgeworths gender their argument: while the common gender noun "child" universalizes this piece of advice, it is really *girls* whose "taste" can be sharpened by dolls and really *girls,* rather than children, who must be watched for these "symptoms." Historians and critics often read the fashion doll as a toy for girls; as Claudia Mitchell and Jacqueline Reid-Walsh (2002) summarize, "(affluent) girls have played with fashionably dressed, shapely dolls for a very long time" (173).

Early children's literature was one place in which girls' potential "love of finery and fashion" could be checked. For example, it is significant that what is arguably the first novel written expressly for children, Sarah Fielding's *The Governess; or, The Little Female Academy* (1749), includes just such material. *The Governess* is an example of a moral tale, a children's literature genre defined by Humphrey Carpenter and Mari Prichard (1984) as "didactic fictions, either short or novel-length, which were first written for children in the mid-18th cent., and which by 1800 were the predominant genre in children's books in England" (358). "Most moral tales," continue Carpenter and Prichard, "consisted of little more than the relation of the daily events of a family's life, emphasizing the children's sins of omission and commission and their subsequent punishments and repentance" (359). In *The Governess,* this process occurs within the framework of a group of girl students at the "little female academy" of the title. As I have said, the Fuller paper doll books (with the notable exception of the fairy tale *Cinderella* (1814)) are themselves nineteenth-century iterations of the moral tale produced in a novel format, hence a short exploration of some of the lessons re-garding clothing in a work like *The Governess* will clarify my subsequent argument.

In *The Governess* (1749), Sarah Fielding explicitly criticizes fem-inine love of clothing and associated vanity through the character of Lady Caroline Delun. When she and her sister, Lady Fanny, visit their former friend, the story's heroine, Miss Jenny Peace, Lady Caroline cannot help but fiddle with her extravagant ensemble of "a Pink Robe, embroidered thick with Gold, and adorned with very fine Jewels, and the finest *Mechlin* lace" (accessorized with a heavy diamond cross), and her pride in her costume is obvious to the pupils of the academy despite the fact that she makes efforts to conceal her fixation so "that she might not be observed to think of her own Dress" (110). This passage fol-lows Lady Caroline's departure: "Miss *Jenny Peace* remarked how many Shapes Vanity would turn itself into, and desired them to observe how ridiculously Lady *Caroline Delun* (original emphases) turned her whole Thoughts on her Dress, and Condition of Life" (111): Lady Caroline's obsession with her attire is matched only by her obsession with her newly-acquired title.

Layering the moral regarding clothing, the Lady Caroline episode gives way to a confession from one of Jenny's fellow students. Miss Nanny Spruce admits that she once had "the same Vanity of Dress and Superiority of Station" as the group's noble visitor: "My Delight, said Miss *Nanny Spruce* (original emphasis), ever since I can remember, has been in Dress and Finery" (112). Nanny's fetishistic relay of many spe-cific details of dress, from the "fine Coats, Ribbands, and laced Caps" in which she revels at home (112), to the much-envied "Silver Ribband" and "Red Damask" of her schoolmates (113), offers an imaginative feast to the reader who loves clothes. However, a moral gleaned from Miss Jenny Peace's teachings quickly negates these narrative pleasures: Nanny is content now because she has discovered that "the Road to Happiness is by conquering such foolish Vanities, and the only Way to be pleased is to endeavour to please others" (113).

This episode from *The Governess* (1749) is only one example of an eighteenth-century moral tale writing against "a love of finery and fashion," and there are many more. While I cannot canvas all these stories here, it is noteworthy that another of the most popular texts within this genre, the early Newbery work, *The History of Little Goody*

Two-Shoes first published in 1765,[2] makes an association between moral worth (or the lack thereof) and clothing (or the lack thereof) through its heroine's name alone. Once Margery acquires a pair of shoes instead of the one shoe with which she begins the story, her grateful assertion "*Two Shoes, Mame, see two shoes*" ([1766] 2000: 21) to whomever will listen not only generates a nickname, but also reflects an insensibility to the finer points of dress which bespeaks her suitability as a heroine for the moral tale.

Gender, the Paper Doll Book, and the Moral Tale

Carpenter and Prichard's (1984) definitions of the moral tale describe the Fullers' *Little Fanny* (1810) well: in this largely naturalistic narrative, a girl's disobedience leads to misfortune, then penitent alteration of conduct. But, while *The Governess* contains injunctions against a wide range of feminine sins, of which vanity and love of clothing are but two, the paper doll books base all their lessons around these flaws. The sartorially-based morals range from self-contained axioms like "VICE in her liveried pomp we often meet, / But humble VIRTUE barefoot in the street," a verse appended to a section of the prose story of *Lucinda* (1812: 4), to the constitutive plotting of all elements of the story around clothing. *Little Fanny* evidences such a strikingly clothing-centered plot. Fanny's initial fall from grace, for instance, involves a passionate squabble with her mother who refuses to let her wear recently bought finery in inclement weather. Directly after this, Fanny's costume switches (rather, we switch Fanny's head to another costume), and, through this change of clothes, we learn of a change of fortunes: a beggar, attracted by Fanny's fine apparel, has snatched the girl and forced her to "roam" the streets "[t]atter'd and torn" (1810: 8), on one occasion wearing a basket of fish on her head. Fanny is not the only paper doll to undergo such trials: the eponymous heroine of *Ellen* (1811) has her outfit grossly muddied when she falls into a ditch in the course of boisterous play, is bedecked with a dunce's cap, then loses her clothes to gypsies and is forced to adopt their garb.

Little Fanny (1810) and *Ellen* (1811) check the sartorial preoccupations of female characters (and readers) by substituting them for more fitting pursuits. As such, the stories are just the sort of "watchful eye" that the Edgeworths (2009: 11) recommend. While Fanny's mother reproaches her for narcissistically wanting to show off her new clothes at the beginning of her tale, the story's ending opposes such costume-proud behavior to learnedness as symbolized by the book. Fanny's restoration to the domestic bosom has her "modestly dressed in a coloured frock" (1810: 15), now holding not the emblem of selfish and childish pleasure which appeared in the first illustration—a doll— but, instead, clutching a book. Similarly at the end of *Ellen* (1811) the sartorial sinner "makes a more pleasing Appearance, in a neat Stuff Gown, with a Book under her Arm" (15), her redemption figured in the literal stuff of her garment as well as in her choice of childhood talisman: Ellen initially appeared "*with a Book at her Feet*" (original emphasis) (3).

While *The Governess* (1749), not to mention the paper doll *per se,* clearly addresses girls, the audience for the paper doll books is more ambiguous. Although *Fanny* (1810) and *Ellen* (1811) are two of the six Fuller children's paper doll books in the Bodleian to have female protagonists, the remaining five have male heroes.[3] We have no way of determining whether, irrespective of the sex of the protagonist, paper doll books were most read or owned by girls in the nineteenth century, and although the sole example of a male-focused text with an inscription that I have located belonged to one, Charlotte Morris, a manuscript edition of *Little Fanny* (1810) in the Victoria and Albert Museum's Renier Collection bears the message "Mast[r] Rob[t] Browning as a reward for his Meritorious Behaviour at School"—the future poet apparently received this (female-oriented) paper doll book when he was two or three years of age.[4]

What, then, of the remainder of these Fuller titles that have male heroes? The title of the 1816 work *Frederick, or, The Effects of Disobedience* suggests a didactic tone to rival, if not eclipse, that of *Fanny* (1810) or *Ellen* (1811), and an early description of the fourteen-year-old Frederick as a boy "endowed with every good quality except perseverance" (5) does not dispel this impression. However, comedy tempers the moralizing here: Frederick's adventures see him not once but twice adopting female attire. Any reader who removes and examines the figures before beginning the story (a reading habit that I will discuss in greater detail below) might puzzle over a sequence of events in which Frederick appears as a schoolboy at his desk, a sailor, an exotic so-called Moor, a soldier, and a runaway with his kit slung across his shoulder, but also an old woman stoking a fire and a pretty girl with roses tucked into her corset. The text enhances the burlesque of it all, humorously impugning the beauty of French maidens: "Frederick Melvin appeared as pretty a little French girl as had been seen a long time at Nantz" (24). The shortness of the cross-dressing episode (half a page, when other parts of Frederick's journey take six or more pages) further indicates its status as a light-hearted *divertissement* that does not aim to inculcate any particular moral, sartorial or otherwise. While we cannot define the paper doll book as a feminized cultural product by virtue of its subject matter (boys appear almost as often as girls) or its readership (which is unverifiable), the division between *Fanny* or *Ellen* and *Frederick* suggests marked differences in the morals attached to male and female obsession with appearance and clothing in these texts.

Paper Dolls on Stage

Little Fanny (1810) and *Ellen* (1811), and, to a lesser extent, even the miniature, comical *Bildungsroman* of *Frederick* (1816), represent attempts to adjust an existing narrative genre (the moral tale) according to a gimmick of format (the paper doll). In another familiar plot device, and one which further illuminates the gendering of morals in the paper doll book, changes of costume incarnate either broadly or specifically ideas of staging and exhibitionism. For the children's literature historian Seth Lerer (2008), "a tension between staging one's behavior for the delectation of others and finding inner virtue in devotion to the family or learning" characterizes nineteenth-century fiction for girls (229). Lerer's rubric of staged behavior versus inner virtue is most useful with regard to the paper doll books in which we find the "staging [of] one's behavior" in abundance: a more apt formula for the books' subtitles would be "Exhibitionists in a Series of Dresses," so focused are they on girlish displays of clothing. In *Lucinda* (1812) for example, the orphan of the title, fortuitously adopted by a wealthy noblewoman, visits a nunnery and idly expresses a wish to join the order. A nun's habit is then produced, and the narrator remarks, "How much she eclipsed the sisters of the veil need not be told" (27). Lucinda's hazy admiration for religious belief (a namecheck of Lerer's (2008) "inner virtue" (229)) is less significant than her pleasing appearance in the garments of a nun, the exterior staging of her behavior. We also have "inner virtue," though, as the moral trajectories of stories like *Fanny* and *Ellen* prize interiority over an exteriority represented as the "love of finery and fashion" (Edgeworth and Edgeworth 2009: 11).

A number of Temple of Fancy protagonists take to the stage outright, and the treatment of this literalized form of staging is indicative. In *Lauretta, the Little Savoyard* (1813), the title character trades her employment as a goatherd for the theatre late in her story, while in *Frank Feignwell's Attempts to Amuse His Friends on Twelfth-Night* (1811), our hero, whose name deftly combines honesty with artifice, resolves to "rouse [his] powers of mimic art" (4) by performing various characters. The spectacular example *Young Albert, the Roscius* (1811) is likewise based exclusively around costumed figures as characters in a performance. This theatrical device lends the whole assembly a degree of self-consciousness, of entertaining play with the sartorial preoccupations of the format which encourages rather than rebukes pleasure in costume. *Young Albert* (1811) demonstrates this. The nineteenth-century child prodigy William Henry West Betty, the real-life "Young Roscius" whose acting career began at twelve and whose on-stage appearances in London and elsewhere generated a wave of Bettymania in the theatre-going public (see Playfair 1967), is the model for Young Albert, as Albert's "Roscius" moniker evinces. Master Betty played a number of the precocious roles which Albert adopts in the Fuller book, including Norval from John Home's *Douglas* (1756), Selim from John Brown's *Barbarossa* (1774), Richard III, and Hamlet. But Albert trumps even Master Betty with the audacity of his dramatic choices: he plays Othello and Falstaff. These unlikely roles infect the paper dolls. *Young Albert* is remarkable for coming with two heads, one white and one black (see illustration 2.3).

Albert's two-facedness places format over content and context, for although the black Othello head, with its crescent moon-adorned turban, is compatible only with one costumed figure, the Fullers persist in separating head from body to preserve the prescribed formula. In further ludic (mis)matching, Albert's boyish, rosy-cheeked head is affixed in his last role to Falstaff's grotesquely large body (see figure 3). Cutting a distinctly different silhouette to the six svelte figures that precede him, this final character hammers home pleasure in costume for costume's sake.

Illustration 2.3 • Falstaff and Othello figures from the second edition of *Young Albert, the Roscius, Exhibited in a Series of Characters from Shakspeare and Other Authors* (1811). The Bodleian Library, University of Oxford (2012), Arch. AA f. 77.

Such delight in costume seems antithetical to the morals offered in Fanny or Ellen's narrative, and, indeed, to some of the implied values in the text of *Young Albert* (1811). The opening précis of Albert's character encompasses his antipathy to frivolous play, his refined yet energetic intellect, and his love of Truth-with-a-capital-T; he is "[s]o meek, so mild, so modest" (3). By comparison, Albert in the verse that follows,

> Enamour'd now of SHAKSPEARE's page,
> Ambition prompts to tread the stage;
> Of ROSCIUS now he feels the inspiring flame;
> He gets the tragedy by heart,
> Enters the spirit of each part,
> And struts, a little candidate for fame. (5)

The budding thespian's strutting pursuit of fame in this verse is irreconcilable with the character sketch we read only a page or two earlier. The point, though, is that Albert will assume a series of dramatic personae regardless of his supposedly upstanding and modest character, and he will do this so that the format of the paper doll book can be best exploited. The physically and morally odd characters played by Albert, like Falstaff and Othello, signal that it is more important for the book to offer the most outlandish head-and-body combinations imaginable, rather than convey a particular set of values to the reader.

There is no sense in *Young Albert* (1811) that this aspiring player should be rebuked for his pursuit of fame or associated pleasure in costume, a fact that illustrates the contradictory fates of male and female protagonists who choose to exhibit themselves. The performances of Young Albert and Frank Feignwell, amusing friends or a wider populace, are positively lauded; Fanny and Ellen's domestic displays of their finery are punished. The only actress amongst the paper dolls, Lauretta, from *Lauretta, the Little Savoyard* (1813), rapidly gives acting up for a more suitable vocation: marriage to a wealthy benefactor. In line with the trend that Lerer (2008) identifies, female characters in the paper doll books must learn to become less vain, less oriented around exteriority, and more dedicated to learning and their families (which are conflated by the return to home as a return to the bookshelf at the endings of *Little Fanny* (1810) and *Ellen* (1811)).

Making Meaning and the Form of the Paper Doll Book

The narrative content of the paper doll book can be read as promoting a worryingly gendered moral message that girls must learn the error of their exhibitionist vanity and love of finery, while boys need no such rebuke. However, the physical form of the paper doll book undercuts this content. D. F. McKenzie's (1986) celebrated battle cry of book history is that "forms effect[5] meaning" (4), a statement which is apposite to the paper doll book. This pertains in part to the requirement that the paper doll gimmick imposes on the storybook: the story must be devised so as to include as many costume changes as possible. Indeed, this formal demand is so pressing that the stories often overbalance beneath the load. When Alderson describes "hand-coloured figures who could be arranged in different costumes to meet the requirements of the (usually preposterous) narrative" (Alderson and Moon 1994: 88), his reference to narrative necessity and concomitant absurdity signals the problem. Muir (1954) goes one step further in his assertion that text and illustration were not created equal, lauding the "ingenuity," tastefulness, and attractiveness of the figures before complaining that "the accompanying verses were often deplorable" (212). The unusual form of the paper doll book affects narrative meaning too forcefully by necessitating a story with an implausible number of costume changes. The costume changes become the only appeal of the paper doll book, its (moral) narrative shoddily constructed, "preposterous" (Alderson and Moon 1994: 88) or "deplorable" (Muir 1954: 212).

The paper doll book's mixture of material components offers a variety of different ways of reading or "making meaning." I refer once more to McKenzie with this phrase, this time recalling the two types of text he posited in the inaugural Panizzi Lectures at the British Library in 1985. The first of these types is "the text as authorially sanctioned, contained, and historically definable"—the classical textual ideal sought by bibliographers. A second conception privileges by contrast the reader's role in "making meaning"; it conceives of "the text as always incomplete, and therefore open, unstable, subject to a perpetual re-making by its readers, performers, or audience" (1986: 45). Questions of just how the reader "makes meaning" of the paper doll book will be my focus for the remainder of this article, and will provide an additional dimension to my preceding argument concerning the paper doll book's gendered plotting of costume and moral.

The paper doll book is, of course, a subset of the children's picture book, a form in which the visual and the verbal work in tandem. As Maria Nikolajeva and Carole Scott (2001) note in the first sentence of their monograph on the picture book,

> [t]he function of pictures, iconic signs, is to describe or represent. The function of words, conventional signs is primarily to narrate. Conventional signs are often linear, while iconic signs are nonlinear and do not give us direct instruction about how to read them. (1–2)

Nikolajeva and Scott's references to representation, narration, linearity, and nonlinearity highlight some of the key issues faced in the negotiation of the picture book. Moreover, the movable book *sui generis* entails yet more layers, what Eric Faden (2007) calls the "balance between the narrative's linear storytelling and the visual's interactive and spectacular tendencies" (74). Gillian Brown (2006) even analyses the reader's "tactile" interaction with the movable (here, switching a head) as foregrounding "the reader's part in the making of the meaning of the book" (358), her terms directly echoing those of McKenzie.

The specific visual, verbal, and material dynamic of the paper doll book is remarkable. While these works originally came with the costumes interleaved between the storybook's pages at appropriate moments (Rickards and Twyman 2000), the utter physical separateness of picture and word (which are self-contained) means that, once read for the first time, constituent elements can become divorced from one another and the word/picture order jumbled. The format of these books works against a stable narrative configuration of words and pictures since the images that should sequentially accompany each development in the story are readily visible (and physically manipulable) at any time. As a result, the reader has a number of choices of how to make meaning, all of which influence the space and time of the reading experience. One could preserve the figures interleaved. However, in order to insert head into costume they must be removed at least once during each reading. Alternatively one could remove and lay out every figure upon beginning the story; at the first reading, this should produce a clear sequence of illustrations, but upon subsequent re-readings (and the children's book is a site *par excellence* of re-reading) determining the order of the figures would prove more difficult. The reader must take care to replace the figures at their corresponding page-openings after each use, or else look closely at each example to determine the order. Violating narrative space and time yet more radically, one could absent the dolls entirely from their own storybook, using them either to illustrate another text or as toys unconnected to a pre-existing story. The Opie Collection provides evidence of such play in one item, shelfmark Opie E 32, a set of ten paper doll heads devoid of costumes and stories. The Fullers may even have encouraged this practice: according to Herbert Hosmer, "The heads may … have been interchangeable from book to book since various copies of a single title often have different heads" (quoted in Piehl 1987: 79).

Of course, there are various strategies visible in these books to mitigate the formal separation between word and paper doll. Some of these are typographic. Many texts, like *Ellen* (1811), provide italicized notes at the top of each section to describe the accompanying figure: "*Ellen appears in a deplorable Condition, her Frock and Spencer splashed with Mud*" (9). These sartorially-induced italics are taken one step further in *St. Julien the Emigrant, or, Europe Depicted* (1812), a rare example— along with *Kathleen, the Irish Child* (1825)—of a nineteenth-century English paper doll book not produced by Fuller. St. Julien, an aristocrat who flees revolutionary France, dresses as an Italian, a Turk, a German, a Russian, a Swede, and a Spanish peasant in the course of his travels, and there is a text break each time a new costume appears, the excitement of the garment/figure registered in page layout and type. Others, *Little Fanny* (1810) included, incorporate detailed descriptions of clothing into the text proper as well as captions: "See Fanny here, in frock as white as snow, / A sash of pink, with long and flowing bow" (3).

However, these aides to sequentiality do not work flawlessly. Cinderella's succession of ball gowns, such a key feature of the fairy tale, poses difficulties for the paper doll format in the Fullers' adaptation. Textual descriptions of two figures refer to "*Cinderella elegantly dress'd at the Prince's Ball*" (1814: 12) and then "*Cinderella's second Ball Dress*" (18) without further specifics. Active attention is required: the viewer must match the purple fabric, white lace collar, and red necklace of one outfit to the head and shoulders which peep from a cut-out window in the figure depicting her coach, captioned "*Cinderella going to the Prince's Ball*" (11) and appearing directly before her first appearance at the festivities. Hence the reader deduces the order of the illustrations through textile detective work, growing yet more entwined in the minutiae of clothing in the process.

From a theoretical standpoint, textual attempts to minimize the rupture between word and picture can undermine rather than promote narrative cohesion. Tzvetan Todorov's (1987) distinction between the narrative of contiguity and the narrative of substitutions is useful here. The narratologist designates "what happens next?" as the signal question that excites reader interest before postulating "two kinds of narrative. One unfolds on a horizontal line: we want to know what each event provokes, what it *does*. The other represents a series of variations which stack up along a vertical line: what we look for in each event is what it *is*" (135). One might argue that the primarily vertical orientation of the images—each literally substituted for the next, as Fanny or Frederick or Cinderella's head is moved from costume to costume—transfers to the purportedly more horizontal movement of the written narrative. The text must duplicate information already given by the illustrations in order to minimize the problematic of the format; text (body-text and caption) and image substitute one for the other in a movement that does little to advance the story, but once again promotes a sustained, involved focus on clothing from the reader.

The form of the paper doll book contradicts the narrative opposition between interiority and exteriority, between book and costume. The paper doll book retains a focus on clothing (the external, the exterior), amusing the reader with illustrations of costume, descriptions of costume, and costume-based plot devices, while self-correcting this focus through the degradation of girl-characters thus engaged. This is moral sleight of hand: two products gendered culturally feminine (clothes and dolls) are condemned while the very form of the book encourages sustained attention to said products. However, in this section, I have used some ideas from book history and narrative theory to suggest different ways of making meaning of the paper doll book. In short, paying attention to the paper dolls and their glorious costumes (a reading encouraged by the format of the paper doll book) means paying less attention to the moral texts.

Conclusion

The formal configuration of the Fuller paper doll book is unwieldy: there is the potential for Ellen to remain forever with a book at her feet should the sequence of costumes be disturbed, and for paper doll heads to be orphaned in an envelope at the Bodleian, simply because of the separation of doll and storybook. However, there is a liberating side effect to such material disorder. The text may present values of obedience, respect for elders, modesty, cleanliness, intellectual pursuit—in other words, the characteristic stultifying (and gendered, in the case of the mortification of the love of clothing and the interiority/exteriority dialectic) substance of the nineteenth-century children's moral fable— to a reader, specifically, a child reader, but this textual emphasis can be ignored. As the paper doll disturbs narrative sense and moral message, "forms effect meaning" (McKenzie 1986: 4). Margaret Higonnet (1987) argues that children's book formats which manipulate narrative sequence "offer points of entry for the child, who can play with the creation of her own absurdity" (40). The paper doll book is just such a format: the separate visual and verbal texts allow readers to decide what is important in the paper doll book, to reorder a narrative should the prescribed construction not suit, and to experiment with different formations of play with the book, not to mention the doll. Indeed, the paper dolls themselves bear witness to such play. Heads, worn from use, are much grubbier than costumes, while the books are often comparatively unscathed, evoking children who privileged dolls over text.

ᘓ

Hannah Field is senior lecturer in Victorian literature at the University of Sussex. She is the author of *Playing with the Book: Victorian Movable Picture Books and the Child Reader* (University of Minnesota Press, 2019) and the co-editor of *Space and Place in Children's Literature, 1789 to the Present* (Ashgate, 2015). Along with Kiera Vaclavik, she is currently leading an interdisciplinary research network about childhood, clothing, and creativity.

ᘓ

Acknowledgment

I should like to thank the staff of the Bodleian Library, particularly Clive Hurst and Dunja Sharif, for allowing me access to the Opie Collection of Children's Literature while I was completing the research for this article.

Notes

1. See Alderson and Oyens 2006: 131; Carpenter and Prichard 1984: 193; Fraser 1966: 92; Immel 2009: 746; Muir 1954: 212; Rickards and Twyman 2000: 220; Whitton 1986: 97, for other accounts of the form.

2. While *Goody Two-Shoes* was first published by Newbery in 1765, I quote from the third edition of 1766, digitized as part of Gale's Eighteenth Century Collections Online (ECCO).

3. I have excluded the Fuller paper doll books the *Lecture on Heads* (circa 1809) and *The Protean Figure and Metamorphic Costumes* (1811) from this count as it does not seem that these works were intended for children.

4. A copy of the paper doll book *Frank Feignwell's Attempts to Amuse His Friends on Twelfth-Night* (1811) held in the Hockliffe Collection, Polhill Library, University of Bedfordshire, is marked "Charlotte Morris Feb.y 8th 1811." For Robert Browning's copy of *Little Fanny,* see Renier 1974: 49.

5. McKenzie deliberately uses the verb "effect" in opposition to "affect" at this point to stress the causal, as opposed to incidental, impact of the book's form on meaning.

References

Alderson, Brian, and Felix de Marez Oyens. 2006. *Be Merry and Wise: Origins of Children's Book Publishing in England, 1650–1850.* New York: Pierpont Morgan Library/Bibliographical Society of America; London: British Library; New Castle, DE: Oak Knoll Press.

Alderson, Brian, and Marjorie Moon. 1994. *Childhood Re-Collected: Early Children's Books from the Library of Marjorie Moon.* [Oxford?]: Provincial Booksellers Fairs Association.

Brown, Gillian. 2006. "The Metamorphic Book: Children's Print Culture in the Eighteenth Century." *Eighteenth-Century Studies* 39: 351–62.

Buck, Anne. 1996. *Clothes and the Child: A Handbook of Children's Dress in England, 1500–1900.* Bedford: Ruth Bean.

Carpenter, Humphrey, and Mari Prichard. 1984. *The Oxford Companion to Children's Literature.* Oxford: Oxford University Press.

Cinderella, or, The Little Glass Slipper: Beautifully Versified and Illustrated with Figures. 1814. London: S. and J. Fuller.

Darton, F. J. Harvey. 1999. *Children's Books in England: Five Centuries of Social Life.* Rev. Brian Alderson. 3rd ed. with corr. London: British Library.

Edgeworth, Maria, and Richard Lovell Edgeworth. [1798] 2009. "Practical Education." <http://www.gutenberg.org/files/28708/28708-h/28708-h.htm> (accessed 9 January 2012).

Ellen, or, The Naughty Girl Reclaimed: A Story, Exemplified in a Series of Figures. 1811. London: S. and J. Fuller.

Faden, Eric. 2007. "Movables, Movies, Mobility: Nineteenth-Century Looking and Reading." *Early Popular Visual Culture* 5: 71–89.

Fielding, Sarah. [1749] 2004. *The Governess; or, The Little Female Academy: Calculated for the Entertainment and Instruction of Young Ladies in their Education.* 2nd ed. London: n. p. Eighteenth Century Collections Online <http://find.galegroup.com/ecco/infomark.do?&source=gale&prodId=ECCO&userGroupName=oxford&tabID=T001&docId=CW1142403810&type=multipage&contentSet=ECCOArticles&version=1.0&docLevel=FASCIMILE> (accessed 5 March 2012).

Frank Feignwell's Attempts to Amuse His Friends on Twelfth-Night: Exhibited in a Series of Characters. 1811. London: S and J. Fuller.

Fraser, Antonia. 1963. *Dolls.* London: Weidenfeld and Nicolson.

Fraser, Antonia. 1966. *A History of Toys.* London: Weidenfeld and Nicolson.

Frederick, or, The Effects of Disobedience: Exemplified in a Series of Characters. 1816. London: S. and J. Fuller.

Haining, Peter. 1979. *Movable Books: An Illustrated History.* London: New English Library.

Higonnet, Margaret. 1987. "Narrative Fractures and Fragments." *Children's Literature* 15: 37–54.

The History of Little Fanny: Exemplified in a Series of Figures. 1810. London: S. and J. Fuller.

The History of Little Goody Two-Shoes; Otherwise Called, Mrs. Margery Two-Shoes. [1766] 2008. 3rd ed. London: J. Newbery. <http://find.galegroup.com/ecco/infomark.do?&source=gale&prodId=ECCO&userGroupName=oxford&tabID=T001&docId=CB3331269544&type=multipage&contentSet=ECCOArticles&version=1.0&docLevel=FASCIMILE> (accessed 5 March 2012).

Immel, Andrea. 2009. "Children's Books and School-Books." Pp. 736–49 in *The Cambridge History of the Book in Britain.* Vol. 5, *1695–1830,* ed. Michael F. Suarez S. J. and Michael Turner. Cambridge: Cambridge University Press.

Kahan, Gerald. 1984. *George Alexander Stevens and* The Lecture on Heads. Athens, GA: University of Georgia Press.

Lauretta, the Little Savoyard: Exemplified in a Series of Characters. 1813. London: S. and J. Fuller.

Lecture on Heads: A Chimney Ornament, for the Amusement of all Ages. [not before 1809]. [London]: S. and J. Fuller.

Lerer, Seth. 2008. *Children's Literature: A Reader's History, from Aesop to Harry Potter.* Chicago: University of Chicago Press.

Lucinda, the Orphan, or, The Costumes: A Tale: Exhibited in a Series of Dresses. 1812. London: S. and J. Fuller.

Marshall, Noreen. 2008. *Dictionary of Children's Clothes: 1700s to Present.* London: V&A.

McKenzie, D. F. 1986. *Bibliography and the Sociology of Texts.* London: British Library.

Mitchell, Claudia, and Jacqueline Reid-Walsh. 2002. *Researching Children's Popular Culture: The Cultural Spaces of Childhood.* London: Routledge.

Muir, Percy H. 1954. *English Children's Books: 1600 to 1900.* London: B. T. Batsford.

Nikolajeva, Maria, and Carole Scott. 2001. *How Picturebooks Work.* New York: Garland.

Piehl, Kathy. 1987. "Books in Toyland." *Children's Literature Association Quarterly* 12: 79–83.

Playfair, Giles. 1967. *The Prodigy: A Study of the Strange Life of Master Betty.* London: Secker and Warburg.

The Protean Figure and Metamorphic Costumes. 1811. London: S. and J. Fuller.

Renier, Anne. 1974. "The Renier Collection of Children's Books." *The Book Collector* 23: 40–52.

Rickards, Maurice, and Michael Twyman. 2000. *The Encyclopedia of Ephemera: A Guide to the Fragmentary Documents of Everyday Life for the Collector, Curator and Historian.* London: British Library.

St. Julien the Emigrant, or, Europe Depicted: Exhibiting the Costumes, and Describing the Manners and Customs of the Various Nations. 1812. London: printed by Vigurs for the author and sold by J. and E. Wallis.

Staffurth, F. E. A. 1825. *Kathleen, the Irish Child: Illustrated with Figures.* Stoke Newington: printed by D. Herbert.

Todorov, Tzvetan. 1977. *The Poetics of Prose.* Trans. Richard Howard. Oxford: Basil Blackwell.

Walcot, Dr. [1810] 1830. *The History and Adventures of Little Henry: Exemplified in a Series of Figures.* 11th ed. London: S. and J. Fuller.

Whitton, Blair. 1986. *Paper Toys of the World.* Cumberland, MD: Hobby House Press.

Young Albert, the Roscius, Exhibited in a Series of Characters from Shakspeare and Other Authors. 1811. 2nd ed. London: S. and J. Fuller.

Chapter 3

From American Girls
into American Women
A Discussion of American Girl Doll Nostalgia

Molly Brookfield

☙❧

Introduction

On a quiet February afternoon, I was doing what thousands of twenty-somethings around the world were doing at the same time—updating my status on Facebook: "I'm preparing to do some research on child-hood nostalgia.[1] If I wrote about American Girl, how many of you out in Facebookland would be willing to talk to me about it?" Within hours, I had a few dozen excited responses from friends, co-workers, and former babysitters. The consensus was that these women would not only be happy to talk to me about American Girl but were anxious to do so. As one friend wrote, "Oh so willing to talk about this!" Perhaps the most significant part of their passion was that I did not find it surprising. I knew the power of American Girl—the "absurdly successful" (Miskec 2009: 157) line of books and dolls centered around historical characters growing up in different periods of American history—and the nostalgic memories one could arouse by mentioning the brand. I have a vivid memory of my reference to the dolls during a discussion in an undergraduate historiography course provoking a collective sigh and whisperings of excitement from the women in my class. However, when I embarked on this study of women's American Girl nostalgia, I did not expect the reflective, critical, self-aware memories that I received. Women's nostalgia for American Girl is more complicated than first meets the eye.

At the twenty-fifth anniversary of American Girl, it behooves us to examine the brand's continued hold on the imaginations of women and girls across the United States, not least because the brand has been credited with introducing American history to millions of girls, and contributing to girls' identity development (Acosta-Alzuru and Kreshel 2002; Acosta-Alzuru and Lester Roushanzamir 2003; Schlosser 2006). Rather than focusing on girls' interactions with American Girl today, I examine nostalgia amongst the first generation of American Girl consumers, now in their twenties, for whom the dolls continue to evoke strong reactions. I will examine how former American Girl players—girls who played with American Girl dolls or consumed the brand's books and narratives—deal with those representations, how they reminisce about them, and what role they think the brand plays in their adult lives.

I began my research while studying cultural heritage studies at University College London in England and thus my theoretical background is derived from this interdisciplinary field that incorporates elements of, amongst others, museum studies, cultural studies, memory studies, material culture and object studies, and anthropology. In particular, heritage studies examines how people interpret and understand the past: the narrative of the past can tell us what an individual values in the present. This approach helps us to understand how a cultural product like American Girl becomes a part of women's identity narratives, woven into their life stories to support their self-constructed identities. As is generally the case when one studies living, breathing people, the responses I received are refreshingly complicated. In contrast to some academics' postulations that girls who consume American Girl are at risk of being indoctrinated with traditional, conservative conceptions of femininity and American history (see Duffey Story 2002; Hade

1999; Inness 1998; Kowaleski-Wallace 1997; Marshall 2009a; Nielsen 2003; Schlosser 2006), the women in this study appear to have had a more complex relationship with American Girl. I aim to show the ambivalence in the women's memories and how they construct identities around positive and negative feelings towards American Girl.

History of American Girl

American Girl (hereafter referred to as AG) has been described as "second only to Barbie" in terms of its domination of the American doll market (Sloane 2002: para.1). According to its website, the company has sold over 135 million books and 20 million dolls since Pleasant Rowland founded AG's original parent company, Pleasant Company, in 1986 as a mail-order business (Sloane 2002). Kirsten, Samantha, and Molly were the first three dolls produced, featuring backstories set in 1854, 1904 and 1944, respectively. Felicity and Addy, from the period of the Revolutionary War and the Civil War respectively, rounded out the collection in the early 1990s, and Josefina, represented as living in New Mexico in the 1820s, appeared in 1997. Currently, AG offers twelve historical dolls representing eras of American history from 1764 to 1974. Each historical character is sold as an eighteen-inch doll with period-appropriate accessories along with a series of six chapter books. AG also publishes the *American Girl* magazine, offers two lines of contemporary AG dolls, and sells clothes, craft books, cookbooks, and advice books. AG opened its first retail store in 1998 and there are now eleven American Girl Place stores across the United States. My study focuses on the early years of AG and the historical characters that were Pleasant Company's original product: they are the main focus of nostalgia for the twenty-something women in this study.

AG describes itself as "a thinking girl's product line" (Rowland quoted in Sloane 2002 para.10), because it teaches American history through its historical characters. The AG website claims that they provide "'girl-sized' views" of American history by retelling a traditionally male-focused historical narrative through the eyes of girls. The dolls' books are also full of morality tales. As the AG website explains, "Gentle life lessons throughout the stories remind girls of such lasting values as the importance of family and friends, compassion, responsibility, and forgiveness." Scholars have criticized this approach: in her book,

Consuming Subjects, Elizabeth Kowaleski-Wallace (1997) argues that the structure of AG's story-telling "insistently normalizes girlhood, collapsing the story of developing female subjectivity into predictable 'normal' patterns" (156). The stories depict girls being independent, strong-minded, or unconventional only to have their rebellious attitudes "corrected" one by one (Miskec 2009: 159). The initial "'girl-power' lessons are short-circuited" when the American Girls learn patience, restraint, kindness, compassion, and other traditionally feminine, nurturing virtues (Marshall 2009b: n.p.). Whatever the message behind the dolls, the brand has been tremendously successful and its characters and books continue to be the focus of nostalgia for former AG players.

Nostalgia and Identity

> Nostalgia ... is a distinctive, although only one among several, way we have of relating our past to our present and future. On this basis alone it follows that nostalgia ... is deeply implicated in our sense of who we are, what we are about, and (though possibly with much less inner clarity) whither we go. In short, nostalgia is one of the means—or, better yet, a readily accessible psychological lens—at our disposal for the never ending work of constructing, maintaining and reconstructing our identities (Davis 1977: 419).

My starting point for this project was to examine women's nostalgia for AG and the complicated, contradictory ways this nostalgia is manifested. As sociologist Fred Davis explains in his book *Yearning for Yesterday* (1979), nostalgia is a "quintessentially human thing," a state of mind in which individuals long for a past—real or imaginary—in a way that affects their sense of self in the present (*x*). Nostalgia "invokes a positively evaluated past world in response to a deficient present world" (Tannock 2006: 454) and thus we can understand feelings in the present by studying how we recall the past (Davis 1977). Childhood is a frequent focus for nostalgia because it is "finished, completed, summed up" with a clear narrative and a beginning, middle and end (Lowenthal 1996: 171). This past is easily understood compared to the chaotic present and we find comfort in what we think of as its pastness.

Nostalgia is also closely linked to identity construction and self-continuity—the maintenance of one's identity through crises. When people undergo a traumatic experience that upsets their normal existence (for instance, job loss, health problems, the breakup of a relation-ship, the death of a loved one), it can cause a crisis of identity. Nostalgia can help to cope with these disturbances (Sedikides et al. 2008; Davis 1977). Specifically, nostalgia for childhood can be interpreted as a search for one's core identity: an individual can create a narrative that depicts her or his identity taking shape in childhood and continuing, unchanged, into adulthood. As sociologist Janelle Wilson (2005) pos-its, individuals seek "authenticity" (58) in their childhood memories in order to give their constructed identities credibility in the present. For instance, a respondent's nostalgia for AG and her assertion that the brand facilitated her love of history may be interpreted as an attempt to ground her identity in the historical past: through her nostalgia, she can claim she has always loved history and that this love is an essential part of her identity that has existed since childhood. Thus, my respondents' nostalgia for AG can be used to understand how they construct their identities in the present by linking themselves to their past.

The attempt to maintain one's identity continuity in the face of change is relevant to my generation, referred to as Millennials or Generation Y. We were in our early teens when the World Trade Center was attacked on 11 September 2001, and those of us growing up in the United States came of age being told that our livelihoods were under threat from faceless enemies. As one former AG player told me, the difficult transition from childlike innocent to cynical adult was played out on a national stage for our generation and was mirrored by a sim-ilar loss of innocence and cynical shift in the American psyche. Just as Davis (1997) describes a "*collective* identity crisis" (421 original empha-sis) that occurred when the promises of the idealist 1960s stagnated in the 1970s, after 9/11 Millennials experienced a shift in the way they understood the world. It is not difficult to interpret our nostalgia for 1990s Nickelodeon television shows and Spice Girls songs as a longing for a time when life seemed safer and simpler, not only because we were children but because America was—or, in retrospect, appears to have been—a fundamentally different place. We use nostalgia as a "means for holding onto and reaffirming identities which [have] been badly bruised by the turmoil of the times" (Davis 1977: 422), hoping that we can find some comfort and continuity in our memories.

However, nostalgia is not necessarily uncritical or subconscious as this therapeutic form of nostalgia suggests. Cultural theorist Svetlana

Boym (2001) describes two kinds of nostalgia that appeared in my respondents' testimonies: restorative and reflective. Restorative nostalgia represents an attempt to "rebuild [a] lost home and patch up ... memory gaps." Restorative nostalgics do not admit to their nostalgia but rather believe that they are engaged in a search for the ultimate "truth" (41). This characterizes some aspects of the AG memories I received, particularly those that were less critical and those that ground a respondents' adult identity in an AG origin story. Reflective nostalgia, on the other hand, is often "ironic and humorous" and is a "meditation on history and passage of time" (49). It acknowledges the impossibility of returning to the past and it is fascinated with the contradictions and complexities of nostalgia, unafraid to examine its absurdities. Many of my respondents exhibited reflective nostalgia and were able to reflect critically not only on their memories of AG but also on the act of remembering, and on nostalgia itself.

Objects often play a role as the focus of, or trigger for, nostalgia and scholars have long acknowledged the power of objects in helping to construct identities. As material culture theorists such as Stuart Hall (1997) and Daniel Miller (2008) posit, objects are expressions of our selves: everything we own has been carefully chosen according to how we see ourselves or how we wish to be seen by others. Literature professor Susan Stewart's (1993) theory of the "souvenir" is helpful in understanding the nostalgic power of AG for grown women. Physical artifacts "serve as traces of authentic experience" and AG dolls can be understood as "souvenirs" of the "authentic experience" of childhood (135). When childhood ends, souvenirs trigger a more intense nostalgia: the object is a reminder that that one does not possess the lived experience; the object represents something that has passed. The souvenir becomes a symbol of a person's past and is used as a foundation for present and future identities. Thus, a woman's attachment to her AG doll can be understood as an act of self-expression and as a link to her childhood past.

The Study

For this study, I interviewed women about their AG memories largely via email and Facebook. Initially, I intended to focus my research on the AG books and critique their portrayal of American history using former AG players' memories to supplement my research. However, I found that scholars had already effectively addressed AG's conservative representations of femininity and American history (see especially Duffey Story 2002; Hade 1999; Inness 1998; Marshall 2009a; Nielsen 2003; Schlosser 2006). Instead, the conversations and emails I exchanged with former AG players became the focus of my study. When I was approaching possible respondents, I presented myself as a peer, a fellow AG fan interested in documenting women's nostalgic memories. As a result, the conversations I had were generally candid and informal and gave me insight into the ways in which adult women continue to harbor strong opinions and reactions to the AG brand.

I am a Millennial, as are the members of my respondent pool, so electronic communication proved very effective in this study, particularly since I conducted my research while I was studying in England. (AG was not a phenomenon in the UK and I needed to speak to Americans for this study.) After receiving the excited comments to my original Facebook posting, I created a Facebook "event" and invited my 200 or so "friends" to email me their thoughts about AG and to spread the word amongst their friends. To encourage some of the more hesitant, I developed a list of eleven prompts that could serve as the structure for a response. The questions were open-ended and designed to encourage nostalgic memories. Some of the questions that generated the longest and most interesting answers were:

- Did you have a favorite or least favorite historical character and why?
- If you had a doll, which did you have and why did you have her? If you did not have a doll, did you want one?
- Why do you think so many women in the their twenties still get excited about (or are nostalgic for) American Girl?

In total, I gathered memories from nineteen women. With the help of women who alerted their friends to my study, also via social media, I received eighteen electronic responses from close friends, former classmates, friends of friends, and strangers who stumbled upon my study, and I interviewed one woman in person. In some cases, I exchanged several emails with an individual so as to clarify points in her original response. Two of the nineteen women were parents who related their daughters' experiences and thus their responses were less relevant to my study. The rest of the respondents were women in their twenties who had been exposed to AG in the 1980s and 1990s. The majority defined themselves as American, white, and middle-class, though I received testimony from women who identified as Asian, Arab-American, African-American, and Dominican. Two women defined their families as lower-class. I have randomly assigned pseudonyms to the women. In some cases, I have edited their responses to capitalize proper nouns or clarify Internet shorthand but I have not replaced words or changed the structure of sentences.

I found immediately that I could divide the responses into four categories based on the respondents' general attitude towards AG. Four women expressed mostly uncritical admiration for the brand; four women were more cynical, with a generally unfavorable view of AG; six women acknowledged the positive experiences they gained from AG while simultaneously criticizing the brand for its consumerism or simplistic portrayal of American history; and five women had relatively neutral responses that often consisted of lists of favorite toys and books. Initially, the responses seemed to be as I had expected, peppered with positive nostalgic memories and vivid descriptions of the women's attachment to AG.

> For a First Communion gift in second grade, my aunt gave me the Felicity doll. I was thrilled; there are photographs of me leaping around the living room in pure ecstasy. (Irene)

> I never had an American Girl doll, but I always wanted one, specifically Samantha. (Brianna)

> I think each girl … had a play written about part of her story, and I obtained and performed the Kirsten one with some of my friends in my backyard. I was Kirsten and I recruited some reluctant friends (including one friend's brother to play the part of Kirsten's dad) to fill out the cast. We performed it on a mosquito-y summer evening, reading directly from the script and wearing cobbled-together costumes. (Emily)

One respondent explains how her love for AG lasted through from childhood to adulthood.

Even after graduating from college, one of my friends and I went to the [AG] store with a few other friends (all girls). All of us, girls in our early twenties with college degrees, drooled over the dolls and marveled over the new ones, the ones we didn't grow up with (like Rebecca and Julie and Kit). That same year, one of my roommates worked at the American Girl store and told me she could get an amazing discount. ... [My aunt] asked me to get three dolls for her. ... They were in my room at the apartment for a good two weeks until I got them to my aunt. I opened the boxes and touched the dolls, still with a girlish wonderment that the dolls somehow managed to hold over me (I was also very excited to come home from work one day and find two American Girl bags sitting on the table in my room). (Julianna)

However, while many responses seemed initially to be dominated by excited, positive, and uncritical nostalgia, I soon realized that my respondents held more complex views and that their responses were more nuanced that I had first thought. Julianna explains how she is concerned with AG's depiction of American history as well as its consumerist bent, two themes that emerged in many responses.

Thinking about American Girl makes me feel conflicted as a historian. ... I want stories about strong girls throughout history to be shared with future generations. I want more girls to be interested in the stories, in the history. I want the stories to be realistic and share the nuances of history. The books do not have the accuracy of a nonfiction book (even one for children) but are certainly more appealing and have more readily identifiable characters than a nonfiction book would. They are also expensive and a status symbol to have a hundred dollar doll. ... Those dolls still have a weight to them, a symbolic importance even today as another generation will grow up with the dolls and the books. (Julianna)

It is these complex, ambivalent feelings that I hope to tease out in my analysis.

There are limitations to my study, not least the small sample size and the fact that I do not have a random sample. However, other studies have worked with similarly limited sample pools and have nevertheless gained insight into the way women and girls relate to dolls (see Acosta-Alzuru and Kreshel 2002; Marshall 2009a; Reid-Walsh and Mitchell 2006). I believe this study is helpful for understanding how childhood nostalgia manifests itself in adults. Specifically, my respondents' memories are a vital part of understanding the complexities of AG nostalgia.

Consumerism and Material Culture

One of the key ways in which my respondents related to AG was through the material culture they collected or coveted. The majority of the responses mentioned specific merchandise, and the dolls and accessories, rather than the books, tended to evoke more passionate nostalgic recollections. It is unsurprising that most of my respondents were exposed to AG through shopping, that is, through AG's "stuff" (Hade 1999: 163) rather than through the stories. Many scholars argue that AG's touted educational value and historical stories are only a "veneer" used to sell merchandise (Nielsen 2003: 87). Even the historical books are elaborate advertisements: girls are encouraged to buy the dolls and accessories so they can recreate the stories they have read (Marshall 2009a: 101). The AG catalogue seems to have been the main means of introduction for many respondents, partly because AG products were available only via mail order until the American Girl Place opened in 1998. Several women remember poring over the catalogue and highlighting their favorite accessories.

> I would get the catalogue and circle the outfits I wanted from each doll. I think it was the clothes that I found most appealing. … I would draw hearts and stars next to the things I liked or really liked. (Renata)

> I remember receiving the American Girl catalog and oohing and aahing over all the historical dolls and their outfits and their furniture. I dog-eared entire sections of the catalog, telling my mom, my aunts, my cousins, family friends, everyone which doll I wanted the most. … I never did get any of the dolls but I would save the catalog until I got the next one, which would take its honored position on my nightstand for me to dream about. (Julianna)

In a *Washington Post* interview, twenty-five-year-old Chiara Atik recalled that girls would know the catalogue so well, "if there was a new accessory … you would find it immediately" (quoted in Hesse 2011).

Similarly, many women had a favorite AG doll based on the doll's clothes, accessories, or physical appearance rather than her personality or stories. Victorian Samantha was a popular doll for her beauty and what Fiona referred to as her "finery."

> I really liked Samantha. She was pretty and had girly clothes and I'm pretty sure this was 90% of her appeal. That sailor suit she wore in the summer book – hot damn. (Emily)

> I had Samantha. I picked her when I was about five, because her clothes and her story most matched my fantasies at the time—her clothes [had] so much pink and lace. (Meagan)

Similarly, respondents remembered disliking the dolls whose appearance they found unattractive. Fiona's least favorite doll was Molly because she "was awkward—glasses ... braids. I guess I wanted nothing to do with nerdiness growing up."

Adults continue to covet AG merchandise, as evidenced by Julianna's description of her first visit to the American Girl Place to buy the dolls for her aunt, and by respondents who recall their favorite clothes and accessories in detail.

> [I liked] Felicity—mostly because I loved her riding outfit, and I loved that her Christmas outfit had an interchangeable bodice. (Meagan)

> I wanted the clothes ... or the little playsets like Felicity's kitchen that you could make Johnny cakes on or Addy's ice cream maker and sweet potato pudding kit. I liked Addy's main dress and her Christmas dress, and Molly's birthday pinafore, and Samantha's accessories—she had a little dog, right? ... I only ever got Addy and the clothes that automatically come with the doll and her little drinking gourd and cowrie necklace. (Renata)

As Julianna explains, "It was a Big Deal to have the doll ... [a]nd if you had multiple outfits and accessories (including the furniture), you were a god among the girls."

Elizabeth Marshall (2009a) found a similar preoccupation with AG's material culture in her ethnography of undergraduate students: her interviewees' reminiscences, like those of my respondents, centered on the "stuff" (97) the women had yearned for as girls. However, while Marshall's interviewees were reluctant to reflect critically or negatively on AG, many of the women in my study were wary of AG's consumerism. The most common criticism women had of AG was the products' high price tags. Dolls cost $100 today; they cost around $80 when my respondents were children. Karen claims that even as a girl she was aware that AG was "expensive" and "consumeristic." Renata's memories mirrored academics' arguments that AG uses its historical fiction books as marketing tools: she remembers reading many of the books but is unconvinced that she learned history from them, commenting wryly, "If there was anything I picked up on, it was the words for clothes."

Some criticism also centered on the American Girl Place stores. This may be because AG debuted its retail outlets after most of my respondents stopped playing with AG dolls and therefore the stores are not part of their nostalgic childhood memories.

> Since my parents moved [to California], I've passed the gigantic AG store in the Grove, and seen little girls and moms/dads pass me with huge AG bags, but have absolutely no interest whatsoever in going in. The sheer consumerism makes me feel a bit queasy. (Christine)

> I work at a major tourist attraction in Chicago and I can't tell you how many little girls I see getting on the bus and walking around clutching AG bags or wearing AG shirts. The American Girl Store is a major draw to the city for families with daughters. Again, I'm not sure what girls (or even perhaps boys) might get out of a visit to the AG store besides new stuff. At best, I imagine it's an affirmation that girls are special and capable human beings; at worst I suspect it's a sense that girls are special when they own AG stuff—dolls, clothes, tea sets, whatever. (Emily)

Significantly, Emily and Christine both had AG dolls of which they were fond: Emily's story of performing an AG play, quoted earlier, was particularly poignant. Thus, their re-assessments of the AG brand show how women have grown to question AG's consumerism while simultaneously maintaining nostalgic memories.

These critiques of AG are demonstrative of women's nuanced AG nostalgia. Although they affectionately recall the dolls and accessories they owned, they now use those memories to reinforce their identities as critically aware adults, keen to withstand materialism. They focus their criticisms on American Girl Place and on those aspects of the brand, such as the price, that they were not exposed to as children and which are, therefore, not a part of their more positive nostalgic memories. In other words, by criticizing AG as adults, these women are able to present themselves in opposition to the materialism of AG, constructing present-day anti-AG identities while remaining nostalgic for their girlhood. The AG nostalgia that focuses on material culture thus serves a dual purpose: it allows women to express nostalgia for the brand while simultaneously playing the role of a mature and intelligent cultural critic.

Identifying with AG and Universal Girlhood

The other dominant theme that emerged from my respondents was their reactions to AG's construction of American girlhood. Many of these memories focus on either positively identifying with AG characters or rejecting AG's version of American girlhood in hindsight. In the former case, my respondents explain how they identified with their dolls' physical appearances or backstories and their memories suggest a belief that an individual's AG doll can reveal something about the owner's personality. Many women wanted or received dolls that resembled them physically, and respondents are quick to draw parallels between AG dolls and their owners, especially those based on physical features.

> I had Kirsten. I think she was my favorite because we looked the most alike. (Paula)

> Molly was my favorite, because I also had glasses and blah brown hair. (Christine)

> Before I got the doll, I knew if I ever got one, it would definitely be Addy, as she was the only African-American in the line, like me, and my parents and relatives generally bought me black dolls and books featuring black characters. (Renata)

> As is customary for most girls, I picked the doll that looked the most like me. (Fiona)

Nadia, an Arab-American, felt a "solidarity" with Addy who was the only "non-white character" during the early 1990s. These women agreed that your AG doll was supposed to match your appearance or personality. Julianna even recalls that it was "odd" that her "blonde-haired, blue-eyed" friend wanted the "brown-eyed, brown-haired Samantha doll."

Sensing this propensity for women to link their identities to particular dolls, twenty-five-year-old Chiara Atik (2011) blogged about the concept that women can be divided into identity categories based on the AG doll they owned. In her online article, entitled "What Your American Girl Doll Says About the Rest of Your Life," Atik claims that if you had Molly you were bookish, "were bad at math, and could concoct various schemes to get attention"; if you had Felicity you were either a redhead or you loved horses (Felicity saves a horse from an abusive owner); if you had Addy you were either "black," [or belonged to] "any other minority," or had "progressive parents [who] were trying to encourage broad world-views in a market saturated with white dolls." Readers who wrote online comments called the descriptions "spot-on" and "apt." The fervency of these comments is epitomized by one woman who wrote in forceful capital letters, "INCREDIBLY ACCURATE DESCRIPTION OF MYSELF."

The company actively encourages this identification with individual dolls. Through the history it narrates, the language of its marketing, and the formula of its books, AG "provides a normative version of girlhood in which the eight-year-old consumer is encouraged to see her life along a continuum of quintessentially female experience," observed Kowaleski-Wallace (1997: 154). The AG catalogues and website describe the characters as "just like you" and suggest that girls should think of the AG dolls as "friends." Emily recalls that AG "sold costumes in real-girl sizes (I totally owned some of Kirsten's) so that you could dress up like your doll." In an attempt to strengthen this identification and create relatable, sympathetic role models for its consumers, AG posits that girls of all eras experience childhood in the same way. Though the historical characters grow up decades apart, they experience the same trials and victories as their peers in other eras. Until recently, even the book titles for each character were identical. The eras change but the girls are the same: they are all "American Girls."

By creating a version of American history that celebrates the supposed universalism of American girlhood, AG simplifies the complexity and diversity that makes the American experience endlessly confounding and exciting. Furthermore, if a girl does not see her cultural identity or physical attributes featured in the AG paradigm, she is left feeling isolated (Reid-Walsh and Mitchell 2006). Indeed, AG's construction of a supposedly universal sorority of American girls negatively affected respondents who felt they could not relate to AG's historical characters. Fiona is most vocal about her disappointment with AG's limited selection of physical "ideals." As an Asian-American girl, she did not have a "matching" AG doll and was compelled to get a Samantha doll instead. She writes, "Since there were no Asian dolls, [the] girl with brown hair was as close as I could get." (It is a testament to AG's position as the must-have toy of the 1990s that Fiona's solution to her dilemma was not to reject AG but to buy the doll that most closely resembled her appearance.) Fiona also describes the psychological damage a girl could sustain if her cultural identity was not represented in AG and she was therefore excluded from the AG "sorority" (Schlosser 2006: 3): "It would have been nice to feel like my heritage had a place in American history," she comments. Nadia, an Arab-American, also got Samantha because "she looked the most like me." However, her relationship with the doll was complicated.

> It was pretty sad ... because I remember looking at myself and Samantha together in the mirror and being jealous of her brown smooth hair (I have black, curly/frizzy-ish hair) and her little nose (mine is not little—it is pretty stereotypical of an Arab) and those attributes made me feel worse about myself. They made me feel in the smallest way that I didn't fit in with the American Girls, which was just another page in my struggle of being multicultural and not totally fitting into any one culture.

Similarly, Brianna, a Dominican, resented being associated with the Mexican Josefina character with whom she did not identify: "I really didn't like the Josefina doll because everyone assumed that because I was Hispanic that was the one I should want."

Although these women all had or remembered wanting an AG doll in girlhood, their reminiscing shows how their present narratives of AG allow them to construct new anti-AG identities. For example, Emily criticized AG's depiction of American girlhood thus:

> Now that I'm old and cynical I feel much more critical of the whole AG empire. All along, of course, there were only some stories being told about American history—most of the dolls were white and they often represented "winners"—[like] Felicity's family being pro-independence [during the Revolutionary War], Addy successfully escaping slavery [in the 1860s] to live (albeit in poverty) in the North, Molly's dad serving (as a medic?) in Europe during World War II.

Women re-evaluate their AG nostalgia and portray themselves in opposition to AG's portrayal of universal girlhood: they are now critical, discerning adults astute enough to scrutinize their nostalgia and criticize AG in hindsight.

Alternative Narratives and Empowering Memories

In addition to expressing ambivalence and criticism for the AG brand, my respondents often undermined the official AG narratives and drew empowerment from their nostalgia (see Forman-Brunell 1993, March 2010, and Wohlwend 2009 for relevant studies of alternative narratives and unconventional play amongst girls). Jacqueline Reid-Walsh and Claudia Mitchell (2006) have shown how grown women construct new narratives around their childhood playing, using their reminiscences of Barbie doll as "pedagogical tool[s] that ... enable [them] to re-vision their pasts within an activist framework" (176). My respondents ex-hibited a similar phenomenon as they recalled gaining empowering, positive messages from AG. For instance, scholars argue the AG stories are designed to instruct girls how to behave. A key example used by many scholars is the character of Felicity, growing up during the Revo-lutionary War, who learns the polite way to refuse tea at a ladies' lunch: rather than engage in unseemly political debate, she need only place her spoon over the top of her teacup. Kowaleski-Wallace (1997) explains how this encourages certain behaviors amongst AG's consumers: "... in this most innocent way, modern girls are introduced to the historical disciplining of the female body: *they* can practice the placement of a spoon, the delicate art of managing a plate" (155). However, Karen explains how she read this story differently, feeling relief that her life was not as restricted as Felicity's: "I remember thinking how glad I was to actually learn things in school rather than learning how to serve tea or do needle point."

In other cases, respondents credited AG with instilling in them interests which they have maintained into adulthood. Julianna says her fiction writing began when she submitted short stories to *American Girl* magazine. I share Irene and Anna's assertions that AG fos-tered their love of history, leading to undergraduate history degrees. Irene recalls organizing meetings and craft activities with tips from the American Girl Club which rewarded girls for completing period-appropriate projects:

> We had half a dozen meetings, each one focusing [on] one of the areas of the historical characters. I remember eating cornbread for Addy, having a tea party for Felicity (during which we learned how to politely refuse tea), having a pin curl slumber party for Molly, and making journals for Kirsten. I loved researching and planning these meetings; the parties themselves were a blast. I credit these meetings as my first expression of my interest in public history (which I now intend to make a career in). ... I fondly remember my AG days as a time when I first discovered my

love for history and making it relevant to the daily life of myself and those around me.

These women ground their adult identities in AG, giving credibility to their present selves by depicting their origins in childhood play. For them, AG was a positive influence in their lives and they gain empowerment from the narratives they constructed around the dolls.

Conclusion

The responses I received show how women's nostalgia for AG is complicated, sometimes passionate and admiring while other times critical and ambivalent. The women's responses exemplified Boym's (2001) assertion that nostalgia can be "inconclusive and fragmentary" and that "longing and critical thinking are not opposed to one another, as affective memories do not absolve one from compassion, judgment or critical reflection" (50). Despite their passion for the brand, the women were able to pick apart their feelings and memories, criticize AG for its shortcomings, and repackage their nostalgia as expressions of their present identities. My respondents continue to negotiate their relationship with AG and they construct identities around their adult rejection or continued affection for AG. I locate this study within the vibrant body of work that sheds light on the way adults use childhood memories to establish a personal narrative and an identity that is all the sturdier and more convincing for being linked to past experience.

❧

Molly Brookfield is Assistant Professor of History and Women's and Gender Studies at The University of the South in Sewanee, Tennessee. Her current research sits at the intersections of urban history and feminist theories of sexual violence. She is currently writing a history of men's harassment of women in public places, or street harassment, in the nineteenth- and twentieth-century United States.

Acknowledgments

I would like to thank Dr Beverley Butler at University College London who provided guidance throughout this project. My thanks, too, are owed to the nineteen women who responded candidly, thoughtfully, and often humorously to my questions.

Note

1. This formed part of a dissertation submitted in partial fulfillment of the requirements of the degree of MA in Cultural Heritage Studies of the University College London in 2011.

References

Acosta-Alzuru, Carolina, and Peggy J. Kreshel. 2002. "'I'm an American Girl ... Whatever That Means': Girls Consuming Pleasant Company's American Girl Identity." *Journal of Communication* 52, no. 1: 139–161.

Acosta-Alzuru, Carolina, and Elizabeth P. Lester Roushanzamir. 2003. "'Everything We Do Is A Celebration of You!' Pleasant Company Constructs American Girlhood." *The Communication Review* 6: 45–69.

Atik, Chiara. 2011. "What Your American Girl Doll Says About the Rest of Your Life." *The Hairpin.* <http://thehairpin.com/2011/05/how-your-american-girl-doll -shaped-the-rest-of-your-life> (accessed 11 July 2011).

Boym, Svetlana. 2001. *The Future of Nostalgia.* New York: Basic Books.

Davis, Fred. 1977. "Nostalgia, Identity and the Current Nostalgia Wave." *The Journal of Popular Culture* 11, no. 2: 414–424.

Davis, Fred. 1979. *Yearning for Yesterday: A Sociology of Nostalgia.* New York: Free Press.

Duffey Story, Nancy. 2002. "Pleasant Company's American Girls Collection: The Corporate Construction of Girlhood." PhD diss., University of Georgia.

Forman-Brunell, Miriam. 1993. *Made to Play House: Dolls and the Commercialization of American Girlhood, 1830-1930.* New Haven, CT: Yale University Press.

Hade, Daniel. 1999. "Lies My Children's Books Taught Me: History Meets Popular Culture in 'The American Girls' Books." Pp. 152–264 in *Voices of the Other: Children's Literature and the Postcolonial Context,* ed. Roderick McGillis. New York and London: Garland.

Hall, Stuart. 1997. "The Work of Representation." Pp. 13–74 in *Representation: Cultural Representations and Signifying Practices,* ed. Stuart Hall. London: Sage.

Hesse, Monica. 2011. "For 25 years, American Girls have been defining youths' personalities." *Washington Post,* 24 June. <http://www.washingtonpost.com/lifestyle/ style/for-25-years-american-girls-have-been-defining-youths-personalities/2011/ 06/22/AG93Y6hH_story.html> (accessed 13 July 2011).

Inness, Sherrie A. 1998. "'Anti-Barbies': The American Girls Collection and Political Ideologies." Pp. 164–183 in *Delinquents and Debutantes: Twentieth-Century*

American Girls' Cultures, ed. Sherrie A. Inness. New York and London: New York University Press.

Kowaleski-Wallace, Elizabeth. 1997. *Consuming Subjects: Women, Shopping, and Business in the Eighteenth Century.* New York: Columbia University Press.

Lowenthal, David. 1996. "The Past is a Foreign Country: For the Motion." Pp. 167–171 in *Key Debates in Anthropology,* ed. Tim Ingold. London: Routledge.

March, Jackie. 2010. *Childhood, Culture and Creativity: A Literature Review.* Newcastle upon Tyne: Creativity, Culture and Education.

Marshall, Elizabeth. 2009a. "Consuming Girlhood: Young Women, Femininities, and American Girl." *Girlhood Studies* 2, no. 1: 94–111.

Marshall, Elizabeth. 2009b. Marketing American Girlhood. *Rethinking Schools Online.* <http://www.commercialfreechildhood.org/news/2009/01/marketingamerican girlhood.html> (accessed 4 April 2011).

Miller, Daniel. 2008. *The Comfort of Things.* Cambridge: Polity Press.

Miskec, Jennifer M., 2009. "Meet Ivy and Bean, Queerly the Anti-American Girls." *Children's Literature Association Quarterly* 34, no. 2: 157–171.

Nielsen, Fred. 2003. "American History through the Eyes of the American Girls." *Journal of American & Comparative Cultures* 25, no. 1-2: 85–93.

Reid-Walsh, Jacqueline and Claudia Mitchell. 2006. "'Just a Doll'? 'Liberating' Accounts of Barbie-Play." *Review of Education, Pedagogy, and Cultural Studies* 22, no. 2: 175–190.

Schlosser, Lise Mae. 2006. "'Second Only to Barbie': Identity, Fiction, and Non-Fiction in the American Girl Collection." *MP: An Online Feminist Journal* 1, no. 4. <http://academinist.org/wp-content/uploads/2010/06/Schlosser.pdf> (accessed 30 June 2011).

Sedikides, Constantine, Tim Wildschut, Lowell Gaertner, Clay Routledge, and Jamie Arndt. 2008. "Nostalgia as Enabler of Self-Continuity." Pp. 227–239 in *Self-Continuity: Individual and Collective Perspectives,* ed. Fabio Sani. New York: Psychology Press.

Sloane, Julie. 2002. "A New Twist on Timeless Toys." *Fortune Small Business.* <http://money.cnn.com/magazines/fsb/fsb_archive/2002/10/01/330574/index.htm> (accessed 19 July 2011).

Stewart, Susan. 1993. *On Longing: Narratives of the Miniature, the Gigantic, the Souvenir, the Collection.* Durham, NC: Duke University Press.

Tannock, Stuart. 2006. "Nostalgia Critique." *Cultural Studies* 9, no. 3: 453–464.

Wilson, Janelle L. 2005. *Nostalgia: Sanctuary of Meaning.* Lewisburg, PA: Bucknell University Press.

Wohlwend, Karen E. 2009. "Girls Consuming and Producing Identity Texts through Disney Princess Play." *Reading Research Quarterly* 44, no. 1: 57–83.

Chapter 4

Barbie versus *Modulor*
Ideal Bodies, Buildings, and Typical Users

Frederika Eilers

ભ૪ૐ

Introduction

"Math class is tough," Teen Talk Barbie notoriously said in 1992. However, this did not preclude Barbie from becoming an architect in 2011 as part of the *I can be* series started in 2001 to promote girls' career aspirations. Contrary to popular belief, not all architects are good at math and even modern architectural legend Le Corbusier admitted in his famous treatise *Le Modulor* (1950a) that he was bad at math. Placing the epitomes of girl culture and architecture culture, Barbie and *Modulor*, in conversation, this theoretical reflection probes the relationship between these idealized bodies, buildings, and typical users.

The story of Architect Barbie begins in 2002 when she won the popular vote but, nonetheless, Mattel decided against manufacturing this version of her at that time (Stratigakos 2008). Five years later, Despina Stratigakos, architect and professor, organized an exhibition called *Architect Barbie* at the University of Michigan. When Architect Barbie was finally released in 2011, her new career was based largely on accessories. She is a quintessential architect from the black thickly-rimmed glasses on her head to the black high-heeled boots on her toes. A sensible ponytail holds back her hair and a minimalist rectangular bracelet adorns her right wrist. Accompanying her in the box are a matching hot pink drawing tube, a model-sized version of Barbie's townhouse, a white hard hat, and a drawing roll file with blueprints (an out-dated form of reproduction). Although many of the Architect Barbies in the exhibit had donned all-black clothing, a common practice of architects in the field,[1] she wears a black short-sleeved coat over a dress that changes from blue to white and that sports a graphic of a sparkling city skyline.

Despite a renewed interest in dolls and architecture, there were fewer than thirty entries for the 2011 American Institute of Architects (AIA 2011) competition, organized by Stratigakos to elicit ideas about how Architect Barbie would design her own house. The winning design, by Ting Li and Maja Paklar, cloaked the home with overtly green features, like a rooftop garden and solar panels (Li and Paklar 2011). This gigantic house covers almost five thousand square feet (over 450 square meters) with its spiral stair case that pivots around a hi-tech closet (Li and Paklar 2011). While the competition was for adult architects, Stratigakos also held a related workshop for young girls at the annual AIA National Convention to introduce them to architecture via their favorite doll.

Inspired by Barbie's recent career as an architect and subsequent AIA competition and workshops, my theoretical reflection compares two dissimilar icons, Mattel's Barbie and Le Corbusier's *Modulor,* which represent similar ideologies of ideal bodies that bridge childhood studies and professional design. This analysis will refresh discourses surrounding spaces built around ideal bodies, yet inhabited by typical users. For Barbie and her home, the Dream House, I rely heavily on the material artifacts themselves, while for *Modulor* and his home, Unité d'Habitation, I treat Le Corbusier's books as primary sources; both are supplemented by critical responses from scholars. There is, in fact, so much literature that a subculture of "Barbie Studies" exists (Spigel 2001: 311). She "has become a standard for scholarly discussion of the relations between popular culture, dominant ideologies, and childhood development" (Driscoll 2008: 45). Likewise, Le Corbusier is considered a pioneer of modern architecture; he practiced for nearly sixty years and influenced a generation of architects, including the New York Five. So many tomes have been written about him as "to run the risk of redundancy" (Frampton 2001: 6). Both are heavily researched objects, but, generally speaking, Barbie research tends to be critical while that on Le Corbusier tends to celebrate the lone creative genius.

Chronologically, Barbie followed *Modulor*. He was developed between 1943 and 1944 (Padovan 1999) and first appeared in Matila Ghyka's article (1948) in *Architectural Review*.[2] *Modulor* was popularized in 1950 by an eponymous book (Le Corbusier 1950a). Le Corbusier tested *Modulor* as a system of measure in the design of Unité d'Habitation, an iconic multi-family housing project, the construction of which began in 1947 and which was completed in 1952. Although the building was incomplete at the time, it is the first of eight examples in the book. Barbie debuted in March 1959; the first of her houses was released two years later. This article's primary focus is on one of her longest available houses—the Dream House produced from 1977 to 1991. Even though about a decade separates Barbie and *Modulor*, they are well-documented symbols which demonstrate relationships between ideal bodies and buildings intended for them. Less documented, however, is how these buildings exclude typical users.

Ideal figures which shape our environments should be examined critically because these environments may naturalize hegemonic values such as ableism. Geographer Rob Imrie (1999) builds on the assumption that architect Lance Hosey and many others have put forward: "One of the critical contexts for the perpetuation and reproduction of social inequalities is the built environment" (25). The environment potentially shapes us to its view; socially and physically we adapt to our own creations.

Le Corbusier's ideas about bodies and architecture changed throughout his career. Imrie (1999) critiques a theoretical project by Le Corbusier which exemplifies modern architecture's ideal, singular view of the user and how it ignores "the [actual] multiplicities of the body" (26).

The built environment, Le Corbusier and François de Pierrefeu write, "models and remodels [the body], loosening this, allowing that to form, operating in a thousand linked ways" (quoted in Imrie 1999: 39). Later, in *Le Modulor* Le Corbusier (1950a) rewrites his initial presuppositions: "Architecture … must be a thing of the body, a thing of substance as well as of the spirit of the brain" (60–61). The rewrite structures architecture as being secondary to the body, whereas in the original he explains a process of give and take between bodies and buildings.

Using this frame, this article is divided into three parts. The first part examines these ideal bodies by foregrounding Barbie and *Modulor* as objects, as sexualized, as modern, as standard and globally available, as white, as arbitrary, and as tools. The second part compares Unité d'Habitation and the Dream House in terms of their material palettes and their programmatic arrangements. Then, lastly, it reflects on how the bodies have shaped their structures relative to the overall unit dimensions, and by the dimensions (or, in *Modulor*'s case, the lack thereof) of functional interior details and furniture such as beds. Barbie's bed, for example, illustrates how her thinness was translated to her home. In the conclusion, the article looks at two instances of how these designed spaces may exclude other users through becoming isolated bedroom communities, restricting the range of family types, and by limiting mobility of differently-abled individuals such as Barbie's companion, Becky.

Idealizing Bodies: Barbie and *Modulor*

Barbie is an eleven-and-a-half inch (twenty-nine centimeter) doll and *Modulor* is a six foot (1.83 meter) man. Barbie's natural position is standing with her chin level, her head and eyes straight forward, her arms to the side with her elbows bent, thus accentuating her waist, her hands passive and relaxed with her fingers slightly parted and turned inwards, and her feet perpetually on tip toes. Overall it is a calm, submissive position. Her face is in equal thirds, as classic Greek proportions dictate. After her premiere, her coy smile was replaced with a toothy grin (Forman-Brunell 2009); and—a recent adaption from the 1990s—she now has an upturned nose and larger eyes so as to look more child-like (Coleman 2001).

Then there is *Modulor*. He is active and he commands our attention. His dominant right arm extends upwards with his hand open, ready to catch or grasp an object. In an early sketch by Vernon Hood depicting the original, smaller *Modulor*, his genitalia are visible (see Frampton 2001). Secondary sex characteristics like abdominal muscles are drawn in many others, but in all images his legs and arms are muscular and his head is small. He appears numerous times in Le Corbusier's books and buildings.

Most commonly, Barbie is unmasked as a projection of a sexualized body, which leads to unrealistic body and race expectations, self hatred, and eating disorders. She is an ideal, and as such, it is impossible for typical people or dolls to measure up to her. Mattel calls Barbie an "aspirational figure" (Norton et al. 1996: 293, 289; Driscoll 2008: 42). But in actuality, it is unclear how large a role her proportions have played in shaping concepts of femininity. She is just one of many unattainable popular culture depictions of bodies. Her creator, Ruth Handler, was a contradiction of powerful business woman and delicate, short fashionista, balancing "emancipation and submission" (Forman-Brunell 2009: 311). Barbie, too, is a contradiction with her obscene duality of naughty and nice, "a simulacrum of a human being, a sad grotesquerie: her creators gave her breasts but no nipples, flared hips but no womb, seductively spread legs but no vagina" (Cunningham 1993: 81).

When criticism of Barbie is extended to an ideal figure of the opposite sex, *Modulor* too becomes a fraught sexualized ideal. Unlike Barbie, though, he often has genitals. There is no mistaking him for the androgynous figures in *Graphic Standards*. This ubiquitous book, which was first published in the 1930s and is revised about once a decade, is used by architects as a source for everything from structural systems to windowsill details; and, since 1941, the book has reproduced androgynous human body diagrams from architect Henry Dreyfuss' research. (I use this established professional source, because Le Corbusier was most likely familiar with it and because Hosey's critique (2001), mentioned earlier, makes use of these representations to talk about the physicality of sexism and racism in the built environment, to which I will return.)

As well, *Modulor* can be viewed as sexualized in his similarity to Ken's body type. Although the statement was originally applied to Ken, they are both "the 'ideal' man from the female perspective; ectomorphic, with a small waist-hip ratio and a large chest-waist ratio" (Norton et al 1996: 293). First, it was a man who created *Modulor*. Le Corbusier, like Ruth Handler, is known for his contradictions. Born as Charles Edouard Jeanneret, Le Corbusier was an artist turned architect. He was vague about his past, attempting to "appear even more innovative and original than he really was" (Padovan 1999: 318) and he appropriated the ideas of others (Loach 1998). Second, the drawings of *Modulor* give no exact width measurements, but the images describe the same aesthetic of relatively narrow waist and hip to a wide chest and shoulders. So it is interesting that Le Corbusier, a man, is the creator of this objectified man, and also that Handler, a woman, is sexualizing both Ken and Barbie. In light of *Modulor*'s similarities to Ken, I posit that *Modulor* can be seen to be a sexualized body.

The two figures, as sexualized, emphasize contrasting distances— height and width. Only height information is provided regarding *Modulor* thus verifying that, for men, girth is unimportant. Consequently, in spaces designed for *Modulor*, since horizontal dimensions are unknown, everything is based on his vertical height. This, too, is gendered. Studies of Barbie's dimensions focus primarily on female body width: aspects like hip-waist ratios are seen to be women's concerns (Norton et al 1996). As I will show later, Barbie's Dream House does not reflect standard proportions; it accentuates the fact she is impossibly skinny.

The history of architectural aesthetics is integrally bound up with proportion, and, with the advent of modernism, the body was superimposed with the virtues of standardization, mechanization, and precision. *Modulor*'s body is a representation of this shift, and the "most obvious modernist heir" of the Vitruvian man (Hosey 2001: 103). Historically, Vitruvius' description of man, now called Vitruvian man, dates from the beginning of the Roman Empire and has trickled down through architectural history, including via Leonardo da Vinci's Renaissance drawing of Vitruvian man. Ideal bodies like these have pervaded our collective imagination for a long time, but these representations take on socio-historical characteristics—in *Modulor*'s case, modern ideals of standardization. His building ushered in modernism through concrete materiality, the utopian ideals it sets, and its clean unadorned aesthetic.

Barbie's plastic body is materially, socially, and aesthetically modern. Materially, plastic represents disposable consumption and "is the definitive symbol of the mid-20th century" (Toffoletti 2007: 69). It was popularized during World War I because of the scarcity of metal. Socially modern, plastic embodies modern parenting concerns about hygiene (Pasierbska 1998; Lauwaert 2009) and so does Barbie. Additionally, she is not a baby doll but a fashion doll and does not reinforce a replication of women's domestic role like earlier baby dolls did; she emphasizes consumption (Cross 1999; Reid-Walsh and Mitchell 2009; Motz 1992; O'Sickey 1994). Aesthetically modern, her shiny, smooth body in the 1959 television advertisement is under spotlights on a clean, modern, white, runway-style stairway, promoting the consumption of "purses, hats, and gloves galore. And all the gadgets gals adore" (Barbie Collectors 2008).

With commodity comes standardization and globalization: both Barbie and *Modulor* globalize and standardize the body. Barbie is sold globally; her body is the same and adjustments are based on outfits, hair, and skin color (Urla and Swedlund 1995; Grewal 1999). The changes that have taken place have to do with her face, joints, and activities (Coleman 2001; Attfield 1996; Driscoll 2008). Likewise, the Dream House exemplifies mass production since the pieces were manufactured at different times.[3] Barbie diminishes differences in race so that the products designed for her may be used across the world.

Barbie's globalization is much like that of *Modulor*. For Le Corbusier (1950a) "the objects manufactured on a world-wide scale with the aid of the 'Modulor' [were] to travel all over the globe, becoming the property of users of all races and all heights" (63). Le Corbusier accepted that the height of *Modulor* was arbitrary, but it was for the sake of standardization (1950a). His rationale for *Modulor*, that the dimension was repeatedly used in classical architecture, is suspiciously based on the original, smaller man (1950a). *Modulor* became a taller man because a friend said, "But isn't that rather a *French* height? Have you ever noticed that in English detective novels, the good-looking men, such as policemen, are always six feet tall?" (Le Corbusier 1950a: 56). Later, Le Corbusier gave a second reason for altering *Modulor*—so that the measurements were simple numbers across both metric and imperial standards (Le Corbusier 1950a; 1955). Furthermore, in creating a standard, the body must reflect a specific body type and the standard person is often white. Le Corbusier had no qualm about increasing the scale from a typical man to an ideal man without changing the intermediate proportions between body parts. This is not a reflection of men in general. For instance, the Japanese men described in Dreyfuss' survey have much shorter legs proportionally than their white United States counterparts (Hosey 2001). As architectural educator Richard Padovan (1999) points out, "any system of proportion [that] can be derived from the human body depends on the assumption that its proportions are constant at all ages and among all individuals" (330). Barbie is also white. Transnational feminist Inderpal Grewal describes how Mattel dresses Barbie to transpose her to India, yet she remains white (Grewal 1999).

Additionally, they are both arbitrary. Le Corbusier (1950a) calls the intervals within *Modulor* "decisive points of its occupation in space: they are therefore anthropocentric" (50). Although he believes them to be decisive, they are still arbitrary; the basic unit of forty-five inches (one hundred and thirteen centimeters) is the height of his navel. Padovan (1999) is suspicious since the navel is not a bending point of the body, but appears to have been selected because of its symbolism deriving from Vitruvian man. Indeed, it is difficult to know where this dimension comes from; in *Graphic Standards* the androgynous figures do not have navel heights listed. However, the dimension is about the height of a five-year old child or a high counter (Ramsey et al 2000). This is the dimension on which Le Corbusier bases his handrails and this could be another reason to mark this arbitrary height since he will need it later in the design of Unité d'Habitation.

Barbie's proportions intentionally set her apart, yet they are also arbitrary in that they reflect an individual design preference, not a typical user's body. These "important design dimensions separate her from earlier fashion dolls, given that both the tactic and movable parts of Barbie were assembled in such a way as to maintain a glamorous pose, however she was positioned" (Driscoll 2008: 40). Health Science researchers Kevin Norton et al (1996) translate Barbie and Ken's proportions by normalizing their heights, and then basing other dimensions on that height. For me, this may be a crude way to propose such an adjustment, especially since she is a half inch shorter than Ken, so why then make them both six feet tall? Some scholars have used other methods to scale Barbie's body, such as researchers Kelly Brownell and Melissa Napolitano, who begin with hip measurements (2006). To summarize, while *Modulor*'s are supposed to reflect a normal body, but do not, Barbie's proportions were never intended to be typical or healthy proportions, yet many argue that they should be.

These arbitrary icons became immortalized as tools. As a toy Barbie is considered a play tool; her outfits were even marketed, at times, as instructive (Pearson and Mullins 1999). Furthermore, like a manne-quin, she is the equipment with which to try-on or construct clothes. *Modulor* was intended to be a standard architectural tool, an on-site construction aid, a system of measure, and a theoretical idea. Archi-tecture is a "process based on standards," according to Le Corbusier (1950a: 37). Similar to playtools, he imagines the use of *Modulor* alongside traditional architects' tools which do not inhibit creativity (1950a). It is these tools, Barbie and *Modulor,* that were utilized to design the spaces for them.

Bodies Shaping Buildings: Unité d'Habitation and the Dream House

So far, I have applied critiques of Barbie and *Modulor* that indicate their similarities as sexualized, modern, globalized, white, and arbitrary, and also as tools. Now I will analyze Unité d'Habitation and the Dream House through an architectural lens. After discussing the role of girl as consumer or constructor, I will show them to be similar as materially simple, as having closed and open program arrangements, and as sim-ilarly proportioned in relation to the bodies in terms of overall apart-ment size, but not in terms of functional requirements like beds.

In passing, it is significant to note that the Dream House, as a material artifact, has evolved from engaging the girl as moving from constructor to consumer and Barbie as moving from consumer only to consumer and homemaker. There have been at least forty Barbie play-sets (Pearson and Mullins 1999). Her first Dream House in 1961—a studio apartment—appeared only two years after she was released. In this house only leisure activities take place. For example she never has to cook so she fills her time perusing magazines and listening to her record player console, because as researcher Jacqueline Reid-Walsh (2008) observes: "Barbie was presented as a consumer instead of a homemaker—indeed, there is no kitchen in her house" (270). The 1960s television advertisement promotes gendered consumption as the female announcer declares: "You can arrange the furniture, and of course, rearrange it—a lady's privilege" (Barbie Collectors 2007). Here the emphasis is on the stereotypically feminine interior design rather than on equally stereotypically masculine architecture.[4] However, these early structures were made of folded cardboard, which perhaps allowed girls to make design modifications. Later the plastic Dream House removed the child's agency by requiring assembly (with its twenty-six screws) by an adult, and it marked Barbie as a homemaker by including major appliances like a two-door refrigerator and a four-burner stove.[5]

One tenet of modern aesthetics is a simple material palette, which both spaces employ. Barbie's Dream House is modular and a kit-of-parts building since many elements repeat. In fact, children can play with it as three separate pieces. Unité d'Habitation is regular in its column grid. It exposes its roughly cast-in-place concrete and, in a similar way, the designers of the Dream House left the exposed plastic free of stickers or paint. There are only three shades of plastic in the Dream House: white, yellow or light pink, and hot pink, but the designers use them to provide variety on the façade. So, too, at Unité d'Habitation where the building's façade uses six colors. Le Corbusier (1952) called this a polychromy façade and he discloses that it was to mask imperfections in the concrete work. The range of colors at non-perpendicular angles contrasts with the rigidity of the orthogonal grid, thus providing interest to the viewer. Thus, both spaces use only a few elements in their composition.

Programmatically, the buildings are similar. The Dream House's instruction manual and Le Corbusier's final plans do not indicate where furniture should be located, thus allowing the user to place furniture. To comment on the use of space I will compare the Dream House box to photographs and to the collage of the model unit. Barbie's bedroom takes up the entire second floor with its sloped ceilings and roof decks. At Unité d'Habitation, the second level of the apartments consists of bedrooms and bathrooms.[6] As with many dollhouses, there is no utilitarian bathroom on the upper floor of the Dream House, but a vanity and a hassock are provided. In contrast with the upper level, the lower level of the Dream House is architecturally confining; there is a composition of louvered panes, small-awning windows, and a heavily slatted door reinforcing an opaque, prison-like façade. Unité d'Habitation boasts Le Corbusier's famous *pilotis*, similar to columns, which restrict the entrance by masking it. The articulations of the lower levels differ, but both discourage accessibility. However, the bedrooms allow auditory and some visual access. In summary, not only is the placement of private spaces within the structures the same, but so is the necessity of the design to convey impenetrable bases and light and airy upper floors.

The overall apartment dimensions of Unité d'Habitation and the Dream House are similar relative to *Modulor* and Barbie. Even though designed for all scales of construction, *Modulor* was applied only to the individual apartment units and the roof at Unité d'Habitation (Le Corbusier 1950a). Hence, the individual apartments will be the focus of this analysis. The units in Unité d'Habitation are a little over 1000 square feet (ninety-three square meters) and Barbie's Dream House would be, at my proposed scale, over 1200 feet (112 square meters). For this study I have scaled her and her house at one-sixth scale or playscale (two inches equals one foot; one centimeter equals six). Both the Dream House and Unité d'Habitation are modest relative to the 4,881 square-foot (453 square-meter) house in the winning design by Li and Paklar (2011) for the AIA competition mentioned above. The floor-to-floor height is seven foot five inches (just over two and a quarter meters), the height of *Modulor* with his arm fully extended; at the Dream House the floors are just under fourteen inches (thirty-five centimeters) apart so Barbie, too, could reach the ceiling. As a result, neither Barbie nor *Modulor* would need scaffolding to construct their houses. In fact, Le Corbusier extols the virtue of using this height so that *Modulor* would not need scaffolding (Le Corbusier 1950a: 124). To conclude, *Modulor* and Barbie relate similarly to the unit dimensions of their buildings.

Barbie's tall and skinny body can be compared to *Modulor*'s body which also stresses the vertical. For this, I compare Barbie's body to her bed. In the *Modulor* system, as a consequence of lacking horizontal measures, he also lacks some functional dimensions. Barbie's body may be standardized but her furniture, such as her beds, is not. Barbie's beds, the ones measured at the Dream House (1977 to 1991) and the Fold n' Fun House (1992), differ. In the latter, her bed is longer than the street lamp is tall! Although Barbie is taller than the average woman, she is similar proportionately to the length of her bed relative to the average woman. Today, the average woman is between fourteen to eighteen inches (thirty-five to forty-six centimeters) wide at the shoulders (Ramsey et al. 2000) so she consumes about thirty-six to forty-six percent of the width of a twin bed. Barbie, in comparison, is two and a quarter inches wide (almost six centimeters) at her shoulders so she takes up seventy percent of the bed at the Fold n' Fun House. Of course, Barbie does not toss and turn when she sleeps so this perhaps is not a problem. Thus her bed may be less functional and more ornamental or symbolic. The bed works as an index that relates to her body; the relationship of her height to her bed is close to a standard body in *Graphic Standards,* but in width the bed further accentuates her skinniness.

In addition to *Modulor* lacking horizontal dimensions he also "lacks some of the most necessary functional dimensions" like those used to determine doorframes and beds (Padovan 1999: 331); items that were already standard were not part of Le Corbusier's "world-wide scale" (1950a: 63). The fact that the *Modulor* system neglects these basic interior dimensions shows that Le Corbusier was not interested in or did not count interior design as falling into the scope of his work: this was (and still is) associated more frequently with the domain of women. In the next section, I discuss how this lack of interest in interior design reinforces how the buildings did not cater to the needs of women and children.

Buildings Excluding Typical Users: Families and Becky

I have indicated how the ideal bodies of Barbie and *Modulor* were shown to have shaped the buildings especially designed for them. The buildings are modern with simple material palettes, are arranged with open bedrooms, are similar in relation to unit dimensions, and are similar in stressing the vertical, but their treatment of functional interior furniture like beds differs. I want now to explore whether these places built for ideal bodies work for typical users. This is the least obvious of the comparisons, yet it is the most fascinating. The buildings are both located in bedroom communities, which can be socially isolating for users without transportation. Lastly, I examine their assumptions about family and disability.

Unité d'Habitation is a socially isolated bedroom community and so, in a sense, is Barbie's Dream House. Unité d'Habitation was the first of four housing projects in Europe. For Le Corbusier these housing projects were not futuristic visions, but were for the present, and were a reaction to both dirty urban conditions and to sprawling suburban landscapes. Unité d'Habitation is located in a park-like setting. Because of its remote location and lack of functioning public amenities, it has become a bedroom community. Le Corbusier had good intentions, but the design discouraged business. His idea to lift the commercial spaces to the center removed them from casual street traffic and hindered deliveries, thus leading to unoccupied shops (Woudstra 2000). This caused problems with his utopian design. "By the 1960s the mistakes of this approach had become clearly visible, resulting in sterile environments desolate at certain times of the day. The dormitory town, which during the day was only inhabited by mothers and children, causing social alienation, was one of the most desperate consequences and became a great social concern" (Woudstra 2000: 144).

Barbie's house could also represent a bedroom community—this time a suburban one. Mattel's pervasive advertising on television reinforces Barbie's natural place within the post-war prosperity dream (Reid-Walsh 2008; Peers 2008). Thus I venture to say that the Dream House is contextual: I can imagine a series of these ordinary, detached houses populating a suburban landscape.[7] Additionally, some playsets depict chain restaurants like Pizza Hut and McDonalds which reinforced Barbie's reliance on vehicles to navigate this suburban setting. Thus, Barbie, like the typical users of Unité d'Habitation, could be socially isolated.

Neither Le Corbusier's nor Mattel's design accommodates the needs of all families. Le Corbusier (1950a) may have had a limited idea of what counts as a family; he cites only four living arrangements: "bachelor, married couple, family, and nomad" (110). It is interesting, in comparison with what counts today as a family, that Le Corbusier considers the bachelor, couple, and nomad as alternatives to a family.[8] The units were not designed for the same number of occupants. The unit at Unité d'Habitation is designed for a family with two parents and two children. Barbie's house is for a single occupant, but she may need more space as her younger sister, Skipper, frequently sleeps over on the sofa bed. Nevertheless, Barbie's house with her twin bed reaffirms her unchanging single status[9] and Le Corbusier's units his inflexible definition of family.

The two spaces also project ableism, thereby excluding users who need the assistance of a wheelchair. Although there are twenty-three different unit types among the three hundred and thirty-seven apartments, few are accessible for those with disabilities, and those that are accessible, are intended for single users.[10] Le Corbusier designed "for the 'good body' or a body which, by implication, denigrated aged and disabled bodies" (Imrie 1999: 35). Mattel released Barbie's friend Becky in 1996, long after the Barbie world was established. While the company undoubtedly had good intentions—the box brags that they donated ten thousand dollars in proceeds from Becky's sale to the National Parent Network on Disabilities—Becky did not adjust well to Barbie's pre-existing structures and vehicles. She could not visit Barbie's Dream Townhouse since her wheelchair was too large to fit through the door (Ams 2011). When I was taking measurements, I found that Becky's chair is not out of scale with a real wheelchair but it does not fit into Barbie's tall and skinny world. At Barbie's other home, the Dream House, Becky can fit through the front door, but not through the French doors. Most of the furniture would have to be removed to enable Becky to turn around. She would find Barbie's dining room table too low to use. So, while Becky's box declares: "they're always together loving each other just the way they are!", Barbie's Dream House communicates ableism. For Becky, the house is not a dream. "Many believe that the company discontinued the wheelchair Barbie doll because it would be much easier to take her off the shelves than redesign the whole Barbie community" (Ams Vans 2011).[11]

Conclusion

By using these three comparisons, this argument provides a new critical lens through which to analyze these modern artifacts. These bodies and their buildings at first appear quite different, but this close analysis reveals many similarities. First the idealized bodies are sexual, global, white, arbitrary, and they are tools. Second, the buildings portray a simplicity of materials and have similar programmatic arrangements. Since these bodies, Barbie and *Modulor*, were the design tools of their buildings, they compare similarly in overall unit size, but only Barbie's Dream House depicts domestic items which reflect her slim figure.

Third, in being designed for ideal bodies, the buildings have neglected typical users in their becoming isolated bedroom communities, in their limited view of what counts as family, and by being inaccessible to people in wheelchairs. Generally, this comparison is significant because it shows how modern artifacts attempt to concretize the body, and thus exclude typical users.

This article presupposes that we should consider the ideal forms of Barbie and *Modulor* in similar ways. While Architect Barbie is extolled as making the profession more accessible to girls, what if, in addition, we told our architecture students to see *Modulor* as an absurdly sexualized body? And what if Architect Barbie redesigned her sustainable house by replacing her centrally planned hi-tech closet with an elevator to better include and accommodate typical users?

CR

Frederika Eilers is a PhD candidate in architecture at McGill University researching depictions of architecture in toyhouses. Her publications include "Making Green Gables Anne's Home: Rural landscapes and ordinary homes of fiction and film" in *Our Rural Selves: Memory, place, and the visual in Canadian rural childhoods* (eds. Mitchell and Mandrona) and "Nature in the Nursery: The Homemaker and Craftsman, 1890-1915" in *Children, Nature, Cities* (eds. Murnaghan and Shillington). Eilers was a research fellow at National Museum of Play and Winterthur Museum, a research assistant on "Re-imagining Long-term Residential Care: An international study of promising practices" a Social Sciences and Humanities Research Council (SSHRC) grant, a teaching assistant at McGill University, and an architectural designer in New York and Maryland specializing in schools and long-term care facilities.

BO

Acknowledgments

I would like to thank the Canadian Centre for Architecture (CCA) in Montreal and the National Museum of Play in Rochester (formerly known as Strong Museum) for granting me access to their collections. I presented an earlier version of this essay on 3 November 2011 at the conference "The Body: New Paradigms, Perspectives, and Practices" hosted by the Institute of Gender, Sexuality, and Feminist Studies at McGill University. In addition, I am indebted to the conference discussants Karen Houle and Lisa Barg, the reviewers at Girlhood Studies, and especially to Annmarie Adams and Jacqueline Reid-Walsh. Lastly, I thank my parents who gave me my first and my most recent Barbie doll.

Notes

1. Many women architects still struggle with the traditional masculine attire believed to denote an architect.

2. Interestingly, Le Corbusier (1950a) mistakenly claimed that the whole issue was devoted to his idea.

3. The Canadian Centre for Architecture's artifact has no fewer than five different years inscribed onto various pieces of the furniture, house, and the instructions range over ten years.

4. It is interesting to note, in passing, that women architects are often pushed to specialize in interior design (see Wright 1977; Adams and Tancred 2000) since some of these same themes reoccur in the assembly of toys.

5. Curiously, of the thirty containers which come with the house, nine appear to be wine bottles.

6. I write "second" although in half the units one enters on the first floor and walks up to the bedrooms and in the other half one enters on the second floor and walks down to the bedrooms. The hallways occur only on every third floor allowing most apartments to span the entire width of the building to facilitate passive ventilation. Although there were other unit types, this is the major apartment type which is associated with the building.

7. The house, with its expressed A-frame structure, is not unlike the popular Lindal cedar prefabricated homes seen in the United States.

8. Perhaps this view is just symptomatic of the time period or Le Corbusier's personal life, as he is known to have had troubling relationships with women (Colomina 1996).

9. Despite Barbie and Ken dating until the early 2000s and Barbie's range of wedding apparel, they have never married.

10. Of the ten different apartment plans published by Jacques Sbriglio (1992), only one residential unit is a single story, and it is a studio apartment.

11. Moreover, on Becky's original packaging she is shown accompanied by two other dolls that are in almost matching outfits, but the differences between Becky and them reveal assumptions about individuals in wheelchairs. Becky wears high-top sneakers and leggings, while her companions wear ankle high sneakers and no leggings. Her bendable elbows and knees enable her to sit without her legs projecting straight forward, which should be enough to enable her to conceal views up her skirt, but she needs leggings as well. This could suggest that she is more vulnerable than her comrades.

References

Adams, Annmarie, and Peta Tancred. 2000. *Designing Women: Gender and the Architectural Profession.* Toronto: University of Toronto Press.

American Institute of Architects. 2011. "Architect Barbie Dream House Competition." 2 August. <http://info.aia.org/aia/architect-barbie.cfm> (accessed 15 August 2011).

Ams Vans, inc.. 2011. "Wheelchair Barbie Dolls Were Not So Accessible." 18 January. <http://blog.amsvans.com/4594-wheelchair-barbie-dolls-were-not-so-accessible/> (accessed 12 September 2011).

Attfield, Judy. 1996. "Barbie and Action Man: Adult Toys for Girls and Boys, 1959–93." Pp.80–89 in *The Gendered Object,* ed. P. Kirkham. Manchester, UK: Manchester University Press.

Barbie Collectors. 2007. "Vintage Barbie Dream House & Furniture Commercial 60s." <http://youtu.be/es1dDVSfAek> (accessed 26 December 2011).

Barbie Collectors. 2008. "1959 First EVER Barbie Commercial High Quaility [sic] HQ!" <http://youtu.be/9hhjjhYGQtY> (accessed 20 May 2011).

Brownell, Kelly D., and Melissa A. Napolitano. 1995. "Distorting Reality for Children: Body Size Proportions of Barbie and Ken dolls." *International Journal of Eating Disorders* 18, no. 3: 295–298. doi:10.1002/1098-108X(199511)

Coleman, Barbara. 2001. "Barbie." Pp. 63–67 in *Girlhood in America: An Encyclopedia,* ed. M. Forman-Brunell. Santa Barbara, CA: ABC-CLIO.

Colomina, Beatriz. 1996. "Battle Lines: E.1027." Pp. 167–182 in *The Sex of Architecture,* eds. D. Agrest, P. Conway, and L. Weisman. New York, NY: Harry N. Abrams.

Cross, Gary. 1999. *Kids' Stuff: Toys and the Changing World of American Childhood.* Cambridge: Harvard University Press.

Cunningham, Kamy. 1993. "Barbie Doll Culture and the American Waistland." *Symbolic Interaction* 16, no. 1: 79–83. doi:10.1525/si.1993.16.1.79

Dreyfuss, Henry. [1955] 2003. *Designing for People.* New York: Allworth Press.

Driscoll, Catherine. 2008. "Barbie Culture." Pp. 39–46 in *Girl Culture: An Encyclopedia,* eds. C. Mitchell and J. Reid-Walsh. Westport, CT: Greenwood Press.

Forman-Brunell, Miriam. 2009. "Barbie in 'Life'." *Journal of the History of Childhood and Youth* 2, no. 3: 305–311. doi:10.1353/hcy.0.0073

Frampton, Kenneth. 2001. *Le Corbusier: Architect and Visionary.* New York: Thames and Hudson.

Friedman, Alice. 1995. *Dream Houses, Toy Homes.* Montreal: Canadian Centre for Architecture.

Ghyka, Matila. 1948. "Le Corbusier's Modulor and the Concept of the Golden Mean." *The Architectural Review* CIII, no. 614: 39–42.

Grewal, Inderpal. 1999. "Traveling Barbie: Indian Transnationality and New Consumer Subjects." *Positions: East Asia Cultures Critique* 7, no. 3: 799–827. doi: 10.1215/10679847-7-3-799

Hosey, Lance. 2001. "Hidden Lines: Gender, Race, and the Body in Graphic Standards." *Journal of Architectural Education* 55, no. 2: 101–112. doi:10.1162/104648801753199527

Imrie, Rob. 1999. "The Body, Disability and Le Corbusier's Conception of the Radiant Environment." Pp. 25–44 in *Mind and Body Spaces: Geographies of Illness, Impairment and Disability*, eds. R. Butler and H. Parr. New York, NY: Routledge.

Lauwaert, Maaike. 2009. *The Place of Play: Toys and Digital Cultures*. Amsterdam: Amsterdam University Press.

Le Corbusier. [1950a] 1980. *Modulor I and II*. Cambridge: Harvard University Press.

Le Corbusier. 1950b. *L'unité D'habitation De Marseille*. Souillac: Le Point.

Le Corbusier. 1952. "An Address from Le Corbusier to M. Claudius Petit, Minister of Reconstruction and Town Planning, on the Occasion of the Handing over of the Unité d'Habitation Ait Marseilles on 14th Oct. 1952." <http://www.fondation lecorbusier.fr.> (accessed 26 December 2011).

Le Corbusier. [1955] 1980. *Modulor I and II*. Cambridge: Harvard University Press.

Li, Ting, and Maja Paklar. 2011. "Barbie's Dream House, design poster." <http://www.aia.org/aiaucmp/groups/aia/documents/pdf/aiab090126.pdf> (accessed 20 May 2011).

Loach, Judi. 1998. "Le Corbusier and the Creative Use of Mathematics." *The British Journal for the History of Science* 31, no. 2: 185–215. doi: 10.1017/S0007087498003252

Motz, Marilyn Ferris. 1992. "'Seen Through Rose-Tinted Glasses': The Barbie Doll in American Society." Pp. 211–234 in *Popular Culture: An Introductory Text*, eds. J. Nachbar and K. Lausé. Bowling Green, OH: Bowling Green State University Popular Press.

Norton, Kevin I., Timothy S. Olds, Scott Olive, and Stephen Dank. 1996. "Ken and Barbie at Life Size." *Sex Roles* 34, no. 3: 287–294. doi: 10.1007/BF01544300

O'Sickey, Ingeborg Majer. 1994. "Barbie Magazine and the Aesthetic Commodification of Girls' Bodies." Pp. 21–40 in *On Fashion*, eds. S. Benstock and S. Ferriss. New Brunswick, NJ: Rutgers University Press.

Padovan, Richard. 1999. *Proportion: Science, Philosophy, Architecture*. New York: Taylor and Francis.

Pasierbska, Halina. 1998. *Dolls' House Furniture*. Princes Risborough: Shire.

Pearson, Marlys, and Paul R Mullins. 1999. "Domesticating Barbie: An Archaeology of Barbie Material Culture and Domestic Ideology." *International Journal* 3, no. 4: 225–259. doi:10.1023/A:1022846525113

Peers, Juliette. 2008. "Doll Culture.' Pp. 24–38 in *Girl Culture: An Encyclopedia*, eds. C. Mitchell and J. Reid-Walsh, Westport, CT: Greenwood Press.

Ramsey, Charles George, Harold Reeve Sleeper, and John Ray Hoke. 2000. *Architectural Graphic Standards Student Edition: An Abridgement of the 9th Edition*. Hoboken: John Wiley.

Reid-Walsh, Jacqueline, and Claudia Mitchell. 2000. "'Just a Doll'? 'Liberating' Accounts of Barbie-Play." *Review of Education, Pedagogy, and Cultural Studies* 22, no. 2: 175–190. doi:10.1080/1071441000220205

Reid-Walsh, Jacqueline, and Claudia Mitchell. 2009. "Mapping a Canadian Girlhood Historically through Dolls and Doll-Play." Pp. 108–129 in *Depicting Canada's Children,* ed. L. Lerner. Waterloo, ON: Wilfrid Laurier University Press.

Reid-Walsh, Jacqueline. 2008. "Dream House." Pp. 270–271 in *Girl Culture An Encyclopedia,* eds. C. Mitchell and J. Reid-Walsh. Westport, CT: Greenwood Press.

Sbriglio, Jacques. 1992. *Le Corbusier: l'Unité d'habitation de Marseille.* Marseille: Editions Parenthèses.

Spigel, Lynn. 2001. *Welcome to the Dreamhouse: Popular Media and Postwar Suburbs.* Durham: Duke University Press.

Stratigakos, Despina. 2008. "Architect Barbie." *Dimensions* 21: 104–107. <http://www.tcaup.umich.edu/architecture/publications/dimensions/dimensions21/> (accessed 10 October 2011).

Toffoletti, Kim. 2007. *Cyborgs and Barbie Dolls: Feminism, Popular Culture and the Posthuman Body.* New York: I.B. Tauris & Co. Ltd.

Urla, Jacqueline, and Alan C. Swedlund. 1995. "The Anthropometry of Barbie: Unsettling Ideals of the Feminine Body in Popular Culture." Pp. 277– 313 in *Deviant Bodies: Critical Perspectives on Difference in Science and Popular Culture,* eds. J. Terry and J. Urla. Bloomington, IN: Indiana University Press.

Woudstra, Jan. 2000. "The Corbusian Landscape: Arcadia or No Man's Land?" *Garden History* 28, no. 1: 135–151. doi:10.2307/1587124

Wright, Gwendolyn. 1977. "On the Fringe of the Profession: Women in American Architecture," in *The Architect: Chapters in the History of the Profession,* ed. Spiro Kostof. New York, NY: Oxford University Press.

Zinsser, William. 1964. "Barbie is a million-dollar doll." *Saturday Evening Post,* 12 December.

Chapter 5

Handmade Identities
Girls, Dolls and DIY

April Renée Mandrona

 CƷᏰᎧ

Introduction

As children, our playthings are an integral part of our real world, as
sensory objects, and of our imaginative world. Dolls and toys become
intimates: we invite them to tea, tell them our secrets and worries, and
embrace them while we fall asleep. For us as children they are not merely
surrogate beings; they take on distinct personalities with their own likes
and dislikes, friendships and struggles. In this article I consider aspects
of girlhood through an examination of popular commercial dolls such
as Barbie, and those that I created as a child. I begin with a look at
textuality—the study of the relationship between material culture
and social meaning—and then move on to consider a brief history of

commercial and handmade dolls within the context of significant craft movements. As a counterpoint to the profit-driven world of the doll industry, I argue that contemporary DIY culture with its grounding in feminist perspectives, presents a space within which the relationship between gender identities and objects is exploded. Positioned within a DIY framework, the handmade doll becomes a possible starting point not only for the subversion of the ready-made identities offered by store-bought dolls, but for the creation of completely new representations of girlhood. By engaging with an autoethnographic examination of my memories of childhood doll-making, I explore how, through this creative outlet, one can play more freely, moving across and within the various planes of girlhood identity.

Textuality and the Study of Objects

Recently, notions of textuality have developed in social science research as a methodological approach for the analysis of various socio-cultural phenomena. Within this emergent framework textuality is not limited to traditional notions of text as it relates to written language: it encompasses other carriers of meaning such as objects, clothing, and artwork. Therefore, rather than conceptualizing objects as operating within a system of fixed, inherent meanings, I will attempt to provide a more fluid account, or, as suggested by Judy Attfield (1996), move "beyond the static interpretation derived from linguistic theory which transforms material objects into images and 'reads' them according to a self-referential sign system" (81). To examine the various and layered meanings of dolls within the context of girlhood identity, I look toward alternative ways of conceptualizing the meaning of things as dynamic so as to replace the static meanings that are implied in an application of the simple decoding process. As physical things, dolls "are used to mediate the interior mental world of the individual, the body and the exterior objective world beyond the self through which a sense of identity is constructed and transacted within social relations" (Attfield 2000: 123). The relationship between objects and people is reciprocal with both possessing a certain degree of agency: the object does not exert total control over the behavior, emotions and identity of the individual nor is the object simply an empty shell or blank surface onto which the individual projects various mental constructions. An artifact—"the thing fabricated by means of human technology—at the same time also refers to the object in the material-culture sense which defies the duality of Cartesian thought that separates nature from culture and form from content, and therefore the physical thing from the idea that gave it form in the first place, or the meaning that it accrues in the course of its existence. The material culture object, rather than splitting, conflates subject and object as a social relation" (125). In making dolls by hand and thus engaging in the creative process, I argue that the potential space of exchange between this object, the self, and the social world in which the two exist, is increased.

A Brief History of Dolls as Seen through Major Craft Movements

Susan Stewart (1984) asserts that while the technology used to produce the miniature object is celebrated as a sign of progress, it exists always in relation to its "antithetical mode of production: production by hand, a production that is unique and authentic." For, entwined with our marvel at the mass produced miniature is a "nostalgia for preindustrial labour, a nostalgia for craft" (68). This nostalgia is rooted in constructed versions of childhood and history. But "[t]his childhood is not a childhood as lived; it is a childhood voluntarily remembered, a childhood manufactured from its material survival. Thus it is a collage made of presents rather than a reawakening of a past" (145). In a consideration of this idea more broadly, it is possible to examine how the major craft movements of the past two centuries—most notably the Arts and Craft Movement, the activism of the 1960s and contemporary DIY practices—developed in response to a society that was becoming increasingly industrialized and driven by capitalist agendas. A return to hand-making is characterized by a cyclical pattern spurred by a disillusionment with social circumstances and patterns of consumption. This experience is concretized in the handmade doll and its commercial counterpart, illuminating a longing for a present that approximates an idyllic version of the past. Different and competing notions of what it means to be a girl emerge, as it were, between the two strata of dolls along with the versions of gendered identity that are considered desirable.

The Industrial Revolution marked a significant turning point in relation to the convergence of technological advancement and individual enterprise. This led to a notable movement away from dolls being made by hand and it ushered in the mass-produced and commercially available. No longer were fashion dolls an artisanal item available only to the financially elite; the continued rise of the middle class meant there was a burgeoning consumer market for manufactured goods. The didactic aspect of dolls also began to shift away from its focus on wealth and the development of a good and devoted citizen (Peers 2004) to the socialization of young girls via prescribed play that involved the teaching of general decorum, such as entertaining and attending funerals (Formanek-Brunell 1993). But the saturation of the market with European bisque dolls and their descendents, the American composition dolls, was not without its critics. The international Arts and Crafts Movement of the late nineteenth and early twentieth century was a reaction against the rise of capitalism and the resulting social ramifications, such as the devaluing of skilled labor, and poor working conditions. Questions were also raised about the "organization of production and ethical consumption, and indeed about how daily life itself was constructed" (Rowbotham 2008: 44). In order to mend the disintegrating social structures, a return to handicraft was encouraged, and the importance of people reconnecting through hands-on creative activities was emphasized. The influence of the movement spread to the domestic sphere and elicited concern over social welfare amongst mothers as well as sparking a renewed interest in more traditional playthings such as rag dolls. For example, German doll maker Käthe Kruse stressed the arts and crafts ethos in her anti-mass production cloth dolls with their simplicity of features, and bodies that were responsive to embrace. This fed a pre-existing preference held by young girls for dolls made of basic materials (Formanek-Brunell 1993) and directed the pedagogical function of the dolls toward mothering and nurturing behaviors (Peers 2004).

Following the austerity and frugality of the wartime era, the West began to see increased prosperity brought on by a restructuring of the economy toward big business and free market enterprise. This movement toward state-led capitalism witnessed in the 50s and 60s was based in a pervasive androcentrism that demarcated social expectations along gender lines (Fraser 2009). But within the toy industry, a field largely dominated by males, it was a woman who, in 1959, created one of the most notable dolls of the twentieth century—Barbie. Barbie, far from being a straightforward representation of femininity, embodied a rather ambiguous identity blending "feminine ideals with feminist principles" (Forman-Brunell 2009: 309). With her impossibly proportioned figure and permanent makeup she portrayed a vapid, superficial rendering of girlhood. She also was tied explicitly to ideas of wealth and ownership as evidenced by her unbridled shopping behaviors fueled by her large disposable income. But while she reflected the patriarchal materialism of the times, she also became "an icon to female autonomy … [and] represented the expanding independence of girls and women" (310).

As the governmental role in private enterprise increased, so too did a preoccupation with overseas military conquests such as the Bay of Pigs invasion and the war in Vietnam. This led to a growing discontent with big structures, both private and bureaucratic, amongst the younger population. For the first time, there was a substantial generation of youth who had grown up without material deprivations which allowed them to look beyond day-to-day struggles and to challenge the status quo through political activism and social criticism. A major part of this paradigm shift was the search for alternative lifestyles that emphasized social freedoms, community and a return to simpler modes of existence such as the hippie and back-to-the-land movements (Smith 2010). Within the latter especially, there was a valorization of preindustrial ways of life that contributed to the revival of the handmade. A number of manuals were published that provided basic instructions on how to do things for oneself, including making dolls. One hugely popular publication was Alicia Bay Laurel's *Living on the Earth* (1970), a hand-written and illustrated book that contains a section on the making of handmade dolls and toys from inexpensive and/or natural materials such as fabric scraps, nuts, foam and string, thus providing a sharp contrast to the commercialism of Barbie and her plastic contemporaries. Indicative of an open and boldly experimental approach to learning, instructions for stuffed dolls and beanbag creatures appear along with short segments concerned with childbirth at home and making wooden barrel furniture. For women, this meant a form of self-determination that could be achieved through physical labor of all sorts, and a newly discovered malleability of the corresponding feminine identities of various domestic items.

Dolls and DIY Culture

The contemporary DIY movement has obvious connections to its pre-decessors given that it is also based on concerns about consumerism and inequalities, but it explicitly defines the ways in which small scale making can enable social change. The DIY movement developed as a way to better understand the increasingly technological world and as a means to empower individuals as producers of their own culture. Simul-taneously, it represents an attempt to generate new discourses and social action pertaining to the handmade and to concepts of femininity. The DIY ethic emphasizes the validity of everyday individuals, often ama-teurs, embracing tools of cultural production. "DIY culture embraces the aesthetic of the homemade, and takes pleasure in the production and circulation of cultural products outside the economy of cultural industries both elite and popular" (Poletti 2008: 32). Contrary to its name, however, DIY does not imply a do-it-alone ethic: it contains a strong social component based on the notion of participatory culture. According to leading DIY theorist Henry Jenkins (2009), participatory culture is characterized by "relatively low barriers to artistic expression and civic engagement, strong support for creating and sharing creations with others, some type of informal mentorship whereby what is known by the most experienced is passed along to novices, and members who believe their contributions matter, and members who feel some degree of social connection with one another" (6). One important component of the DIY ethic which has begun to develop more recently is known as critical making—creating that is combined with a critical assessment of materials, designs and outcomes. It is through the act of critical making that DIYers can actively (re)construct and communicate ideas about the DIY object and the identities created with and through that ob-ject. DIY has developed against the backdrop of current neoliberalism: the efforts of industry have begun to lead to the disenfranchisement of the working class. More and more jobs have been shifted away from hands-on work toward the service and technology sectors, and the ma-jority of manufacturing processes have been shipped overseas where labor costs are low. This has meant that the corporate elite now largely control the means of production. Consumer goods as an effective me-dium for the distribution of information to consumers, in turn, reflects this change. The doll manufacturers of the new millennium have taken advantage of this "time of exponential information and textual growth" (Carrington 2003: 96). Contemporary dolls are not limited to material accessories but extend into a world of intertextuality between objects, books, websites, videos chat rooms, games and advertisements. While today's dolls, such as those of the popular big-headed varieties (such as Bratz, Liv, My Scene) reflect more traditional notions of femininity they also embody a newer subjectivity, one that is based on fun, on what is perceived to be sexiness, and on a promise of diversity. For example, the video montages on the livworld.com website introduce the four Liv dolls one by one with lines like "Hey! Alexis in the house! She lives for fashion. And loves to dress her friends." A recent internet hub page announcing the dolls stated that "with these four ladies, you're bound to find one that matches your girl best" (HubPages 2010: 1).

As a current maker of dolls who also grew up making dolls as a girl, I am suggesting that there is great potential for handmade dolls to be positioned within a DIY framework so as to provide a counterpoint to current forms of doll consumerism. Through the making of handmade dolls, girls can be brought more fully into the production of knowledge at the level of object creation, not only through use or play. This in turn might enable girls to be repositioned as more active participants (or cultural agents) in the creation and (re)creation of meanings enacted by dolls and, ultimately, girlhood identities—both individual and collective.

In his book on DIY craft, *Bazaar Bizarre: Not Your Granny's Crafts* (2005) Greg Der Ananian states that crafters "can figuratively and literally cut the ties that bind us to the notion that crafts are quiet or weak. The predictably precious imagery of commercialized decorative crafting only fosters the lame sexist ideas surrounding traditional handicrafts and their worth in a culture that wants to keep crafts in a very specific devalued pocket of representation" (120). By embracing the homemade and creative resistance, DIY positions itself within feminist discourses, more specifically third wave feminist critiques of consumer culture and normative femininity. Third wave feminism focuses on female empowerment (economic, political and personal). There is also an emphasis on the use of personal empowerment as a starting point for societal change. Recent discussions of girlhood identity have identified the "defining of the 'third wave' within feminist discourses as an important site for examining those assumptions impacting the constitution of 'girl' subjects within feminisms" (Eisenhauer 2004: 81). Thus, engagement with this form of feminist pedagogy is useful, not only for examining the multivocal and often contradictory girl subject, but as a potential means for girls to navigate dominant femininities (Harris 2004). As Mitchell and Reid-Walsh (2002) contend, "the act of handling the commodified emblems of conventional, Western femininity in a leisure activity has provided, and continues to provide, girls with a way to literally and conceptually manipulate the concept of commodified homogenous womanhood" (202). By taking this a step further—beyond handling to creating—perhaps it becomes possible for girls themselves to deconstruct and construct girlhood identities beyond those performed through today's commercially available dolls.

Looking Back: Memory Work and Children's Material Culture

Memory work, an emergent method within the field of childhood studies, uses adult remembering as a means of investigating the relationship between children and the material world. Mitchell and Reid-Walsh (2002) suggest that, "far from regarding memory work as a corrective strategy ('after all what can children know'), we see it as giving researchers access to components of the 'afterlife' of childhood that are not otherwise available, either ethically or conceptually" (56). This approach is based on the premise that "memory is a process, an activity, a construct; and that memory has social and cultural as well as personal resonance" (Kuhn 2010: 298). It is fairly obvious that memory is far from infallible. However, the use of adult memory work becomes important since, although certain historical objects may still exist to be looked at, touched and smelled, as keepsakes they are no longer played with or talked to, so a retrospective interrogation into this secret life becomes necessary. Aspects of material culture such as objects, photos and films from our childhood past become a portal through which we may access a time when we shared a different form of connection to the sensory world around us. Remembering back to our childhood includes remembering how the divisions between living and inanimate objects, such as dolls, were blurred, and this is to remember how closely these objects are connected to life and to the child psyche but also how they help to shape childhood selves in relation to those around us. Drawing on the work of scholars such as Annette Kuhn (1995; 2010) and Mitchell and Reid-Walsh (2002) I create a form of memory text around my handmade dolls and how they relate to the formation of my sense of being a girl. Revisiting my childhood home where artifacts of my earlier life remain on shelves and in boxes, I begin with the physical objects themselves and engage in acts of "deliberate remembering" (Mitchell 2010: 98) using the sensory properties of the dolls as triggers for their purpose, method of creation, and use within a specific context. In making handmade dolls, I was present for the entire life course of each doll, from conception to use, from initial states as blobs of stuffing and bits of string, to more substantial forms that then gave rise to unique characteristics and personalities. Creating a doll from scratch creates a complexity of memories because there is an engagement with multiple aspects of the self—creative, physical, emotional. This process offers something different from getting a store-bought doll: one you make yourself also becomes associated with memories of accomplishment and mastery over materials.

My Childhood Handmade Doll and its Counterpart

To retell snippets of my past and my connection to dolls as material objects I must first begin with an account of a time when I did not yet exist. My parents had immigrated to Canada from the United States in the 1970s during the Vietnam War, creating a substantial physical as well as psychological distance between their respective families. My mother came from Connecticut with her first husband, a conscientious objector. My California-born father went AWOL after receiving his army medic training but before he was to be shipped to Vietnam. Following my mother's divorce, my parents met and settled in southeastern New Brunswick, having borrowed money to purchase a 500 acre plot of undeveloped land. They, along with a small number of Canadians and other expat Americans, formed a back-to-the-land community, with the aim of providing for themselves, and living off what the land offered. This included growing their own food, building their own homes and supporting themselves financially through the development of trades and hands-on skills. This return to nature and a less complicated existence fed their longing for the pre-industrial and their rejection of the ongoing concern with national opulence and mobility. The new lifestyle choice of my parents represented for them an escape from what they saw as the materialism of their childhood, an escape from the social pressures of the 1950s, a time when, in the words of my father, as I remember them, "wealth outweighed imagination." Indeed, during the post-war years short-sighted optimism abounded as pundits claimed instantaneous economic prosperity and energy costs too cheap to meter (Brown 2011).

Although my parents had decided to distance themselves from certain aspects of the commercialized world—they avoided hallmarks of popular culture such as television—born, as I was, in 1984 I was exposed to many contemporary store-bought dolls. Most of these dolls that I owned as a child came from the female relatives on my mother's side of the family. They were picked out for me by my aunt and grandmother and came in the mail as gifts for Christmas and birthdays. They were of two popular varieties, the porcelain and the Barbie doll (see illustrations 5.1 and 5.2). They signified important life and social events, celebrations that typically involve a family presence, but these miniature bodies offered a tenuous connection to the relatives I rarely saw and knew little about. I did, however, play readily with them. The porcelain dolls were designed as collectables rather than playthings but the distance created by keeping them shelved was unsettling to me. One of the first porcelain dolls I received was dressed in a replica turn-of-the-century dress and bonnet in a pink floral print and, upon her arrival at Christmas, my wooden doll cradle was designated as hers despite her older appearance. I proceeded to instruct my mother to write out the name that I had made up for her in large block letters on a piece of note paper—KABATICA—which I taped to the inside of the crib so that, in my words, I would "always remember." This placed her in the position of a child and made me the adult who, upon what I thought of as her birth or arrival at Christmas, I named and proceeded to take care of, rocking her to sleep in her cradle. After I toted her around for some time and performed a few alterations such as cutting a slit down the back of her dress and sewing on a strip of Velcro so that I could change her clothes because she would often accompany me outdoors, eventually Kabatica's inflexibility led to her deterioration and her placement back on the shelf with the other porcelain dolls. In order that she retain some of her original tidy appearance I first cut the large mat

Illustration 5.1 • Barbie dolls, circa 1987 to 1998. Private collection.

that her pipe curls had become and thus created a much shorter bob. Kabatica and the other porcelain dolls represented the lack of a deep or prolonged emotional connection—a space of incompleteness—for they were not designed with the needs and desires of a young user in mind. Also they were not picked out by my relatives (who all resided in large cities) to fit in with my rural lifestyle and tendencies toward outdoor play. The porcelain dolls of my childhood in the 1980s and 1990s were a throwback to many of the earlier versions with period dress and infantilized physical features but which still carried with them socially prescribed meanings and specific patterns of use such as the promotion of mothering behaviors. Despite my attempts at disrupting the quiet compliance of these dolls with outdoor use and clothing alterations, it was a confined space to operate within and ultimately they remained tethered to an identity of pretty, precious things to be looked at.

Illustration 5.2 • Porcelain dolls. Private collection.

As an only child who was schooled at home, I spent a good deal of time engaged in solitary doll play. But it was when I was with my friends that the Barbies were brought out. All of the Barbie, Skipper and Ken iterations were kept in a large plastic Tupperware container that we would reach into to pick which we wanted. More often than not, we simply picked the one that was best suited to what we wanted to do. So, it was Ice Capades Barbie who accompanied us outside in winter to play in the snow and skate on frozen puddles. The activity of skating was a difficult thing to get Barbie to do because of her permanent tiptoe foot position and her skimpy skating outfit was a cause for concern in sub-zero Canadian temperatures. There were also some favorite Barbies designated as such not because of their vocation or life role, but because they managed to stand out from the heap of shiny flesh, such as a bridal Barbie with distinctly reddish hair. Ruth (my oldest childhood friend who also happened to have red hair) and I would vie for the use of this doll possibly because of our desire to be celebrated for our differences rather than being ridiculed by our peers. But usually this bride would be stripped of her gown and the over-sized diamond ring popped out of the hole in her hand to be exchanged for outfits more suited to varied activities like the ones we ourselves engaged in as young girls. It is this type of versatility that lies behind Barbie's appeal. As noted by Lynn Spigel (2001), in the doll's world "there is room enough for almost anyone's fantasy" (311). It was within Barbie's being generic that the prescribed boundaries of gendered identities put forward by my dolls were pushed at, their narratives personalized. But pre-packaged fantasy has its limitations—in this case it is largely self-contained and as a result came up short. Instead, my own inadequacy in attempting to influence how others saw me was underlined, despite repeating the Barbie mantra "I can be anything." Barbie moves through her multiple identities with apparent ease, becoming anything at will. But for young girls like myself then, reality was often less flexible and possession of the identities that I yearned to embody was far more difficult because in order to be viable these selves had to be recognized and accepted by others in the social world around me. So no matter how much I worked at being identified as the funny, clever and engaging girl, to many of my peers it seemed I was still that weird girl who was home-schooled and who lived in the woods with her hippie parents, and no TV.

Figure 3 • Cloth doll, made by April (eight years-old). Cloth, beads.

Figure 4 • Flower doll, made by April (twelve years-old). Clay, silk flowers, cloth.

Both my mother and father were well-provided for as children but a lack of communication and understanding between them and their parents created rifts early on. The absence of meaningful connection and perhaps a yearning for a past that they themselves had not experienced led my parents to stress the importance of the parent-child relationship during my upbringing. Home-schooled until the age of ten, I spent a great deal of time engaged in creative activities with my parents. Being the only child of two self-employed people and living in rural seclusion also offered ample time for guided and independent creative explora-tion. During this time, I made dolls and other related materializations such as anthropomorphic creatures more than any other object. It was my mother who was my primary source of knowledge regarding the so-

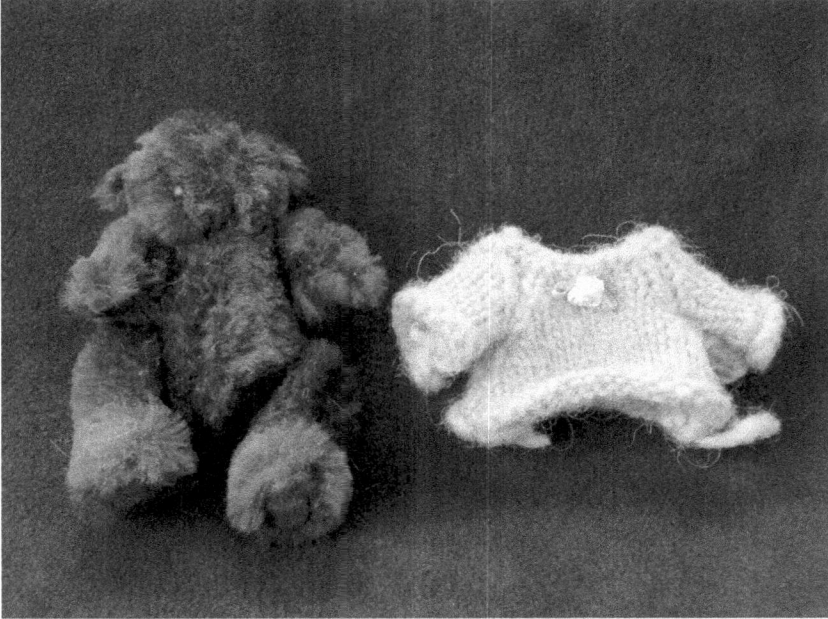

Figure 5 • Teddy with knit sweater, made by April (fourteen years-old). Faux fur, yarn, ribbon.

called feminine pursuits such as sewing, crocheting and knitting and it was by using these skills that I created my first doll forms. I first learned to sew by hand and follow small patterns we cut out of typing paper. The first attempts were somewhat clumsy, the patterns cut in a way that resembled bloated stick people, making the dolls appear as if they were frozen in various calisthenic positions. Then my mother introduced me to the Singer sewing machine and we used patterns photocopied from library books or picked out of the Simplicity catalogue. These provided basic blueprints and methods of construction which could be adapted to suit a specific vision. This was a form of learning based on shared active and prolonged engagement between my mother and me but it also formed the basis for self-teaching. I began to expand into other media working my way through books on papier maché and clay. I made mixed media dolls from fabric, string, wood, and the occasional dried apple or corn husk (see illustrations 5.3, 5.4, and 5.5). It was through this intimate act of making and skill sharing that I developed independence and resourcefulness but also participated in a network of social relationships. This in turn contributed to both the conscious and unconscious messages the homemade dolls conveyed for they became surfaces of possibility which could evolve and expand in various directions depending on the medium, construction technique and imagery employed. It was not that the dolls did not make reference to indicators of normative gender identities such as particular styles of dress or body features like made-up faces but they were closer to projections of my inner world.

Some of the dolls that I made I kept to play with or to use as decorative pieces, such as the fairies (see illustration 5.6), but a significant portion of them I gave as gifts, mostly to the women in my family. When I was around ten years of age, my grandmother developed a fascination with angel imagery. This led to my making a series of angel dolls for her, which came in the form of a Native American, a sculpted self-portrait, a teddybear, and a chicken, for example. The chicken angel was modeled after one of my most beloved childhood toys—Bunny—a cotton rabbit made by my mother's friend. Growing up during the Depression, my grandmother had to leave school at the age of fifteen to work in a factory. This was the result of finding her father attempting suicide, an act motivated by the belief that in his jobless state the family would be better off without him. A general scarcity of money to put toward frivolities such as toys and then having to work full-time to supplement the family income, excluded my grandmother from many experiences of childhood. The spoiling of me as her granddaughter through material things was, I think, in part an attempt to account for her own childhood deprivations but also a way to rectify the shortcomings in the relationships she had with her own children. Although my grandmother gave me most of my store-bought dolls, the act of exchanging homemade versions with her had more resonance. Making things with my grandmother on my yearly visits represent some of the few memories I have of her as active and engaged. When I was perhaps eight or nine years of age I arrived at my grandmother's house to find a small puppet theatre, constructed from a cardboard box and fabric remnants, in the basement. She had been looking after one of the neighbor girls and she sat with us on the floor playing and helping to glue together bits of household items into puppets used to animate the theatre.

In addition to giving away homemade dolls, I also sold them in my mother's craft store where I had set up a miniature version of the sales counter from some plinths and black velvet. I attached pins to small dolls (see illustration 5.7) so that they could be worn but I also

Illustration 5.6 • Fairy queen, made by April (thirteen years-old). Clay, fabric, wool, acrylic, jewellery findings.

had stand-alone pieces, some made from repurposed items like old 35mm film canisters. The activities of gift-giving and doll-selling situated me as an active participant in the regulation of cross-generational relationships as well as within the larger social spheres of production and exchange, providing me with a new-found sense of agency. This

Illustration 5.7 • Toothpick dolls, made by April (ten years-old).
Toothpicks, embroidery floss, glue.

situation recalls Lynn Spigel's (2001) comments about the socially constructed meaning of objects and the relation of traditionally disempowered groups to them. She suggests that artisan labor, as an activity performed by women, plays a central role in the assignment of new value to objects previously devalued in the larger systems of power. It is through the gendered and relational practice of craft that women influence both the cultural and economic currency of objects in contemporary capitalist society.

This anachronistic approach to changing, not only the identity of craft objects but also that of their makers, stands in contrast to the popular affirmation of female culture—girl power—that was surfacing during my childhood. This was a call to arms for girls to embrace the power of their femininity and assert themselves as capable and independent individuals. However, for all its exuberance the girl power discourse said very little about what it actually took to become a strong, self-made women of the times (Charles 2010). This is reminiscent of the proclamations of Barbie, who, by the time I was a teenybopper, had become a poster doll for the girl power movement with unlimited wealth generated by glamorous careers. For although Barbie was a surgeon, a pilot, and a world leader before real women had the opportunity to fill these roles, the struggles that women endured to gain rights and recognition largely fail to make it into her popular narrative. The easy jump between wanting something, trying it out and enjoying huge success suggests pre-fabricated rather than self-generated empowerment. This is ultimately a empty gesture and overlooks the ways in which girls can achieve actualization through practices that are often subtle but creative and innovative.

Looking Forward: Expanding the DIY Doll Community

As part of an ongoing doctoral project working with both high school and elementary students in an under-resourced area of rural South Africa, I have attempted to co-create communities of artistic practice. The region is largely farmland dotted with informally segregated communities of mostly black residents who are still experiencing the shifting and unsettled social and economic repercussions of the end of Apartheid. Although this context is far removed from that of my own girlhood, I draw on forms of resourcefulness and reciprocal learning I accrued from my early experiments with art-making. By recounting my own remembered acts of doll-making to map out my interest in the subject, a process referred to by Jane Miller (1995) as "the autobiography of the question" (23), I have begun to develop a language which helps to express my new experiences and which can speak to the stories of my participants. Together with the girls, I have begun an interrogation of their surroundings in an effort to identify materials and techniques that offer possibilities for artistic expression. This has included the collection of various recycled, repurposed or naturally available items that can be used to make things such as dolls. The girls gather, from their own homes and neighborhoods, bits of fabric that they have salvaged from old clothes that they then cut apart and reconstruct into various human-like forms (see illustration 5.8). We also dig clay from the nearby rivers which is then dried in the sun, ground on stones, reconstituted, shaped and sawdust-fired. They often bring with them artworks or ideas that they worked on independently and then share these with the group. Together the girls instill new social value into base materials, and they develop practical skills.

Both sewing and ceramics are identified as feminine activities within the South African Zulu culture (Gaitskell 1999; Vincentelli 2003). However, they also represent a connection to a history of craft that has begun to disappear. Because of the HIV/AIDS epidemic that is compounded by poverty, lack of education, and lack of opportunity in rural areas in particular, entire generations have been ravaged. According to the most recent National Department of Health report (2011), the HIV rate among the general population in KwaZulu-Natal is 25.0%, higher than in any other South African province. Rates among the female populations tend to be higher still with individuals aged between fifteen and fifty-nine years exhibiting infection rates as high as 43.0% (Ramjee et al. 2011). Dying with these women is the transmission of hands-on skills and cultural knowledges to successors. Thus, our making of dolls and other acts of creation become forms of cultural remembrance, reaching back into the past to grasp at an artistic heritage. But at the same time, this form of recollection forces a redefinition

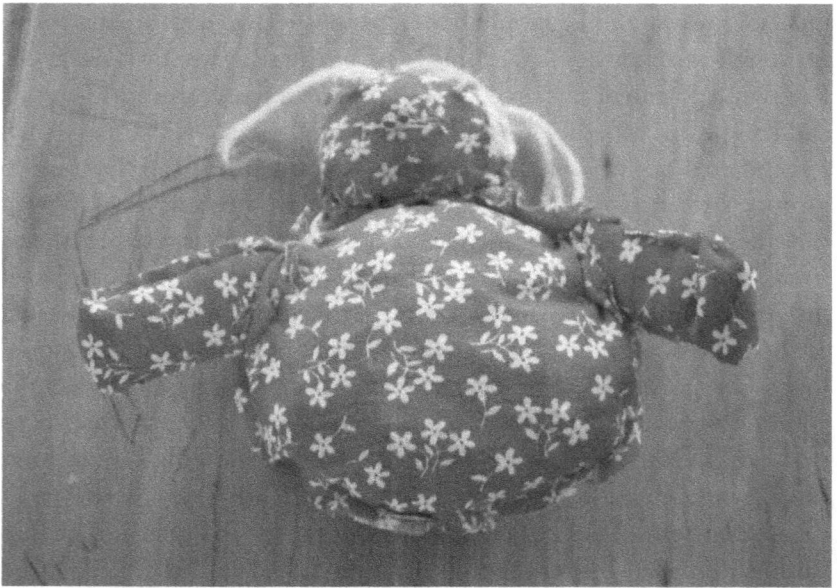

Illustration 5.8 • Recycled cloth doll stuffed with refuse. Zulu girl (fifteen years-old).

of the meaning embedded in both the creative process and the product. Using what is at hand in the immediate environment to create dolls, not only alters the identity of the spaces where these girls live but it illustrates the potential power they have as girls and how they can push the boundaries of representations of girlhood. Judith Butler's theory of the construction of gendered identities through things is useful for the discussion of such an application. According to Butler (2004), gender, despite its pervasive nature, is ultimately a social construction and therefore changeable. However, she also cautions that the ability to question gender is not to be confused with some form of Godlike power over one's external social constitution but that a certain degree of agency is possible. In other words, "The 'I' ... finds itself at once constituted by norms and dependent on them but also endeavors to live in ways that maintains a critical and transformative relation to them" (3). These girls have creative power and skills which they use to conjure up aspects of childhood often unavailable to them. The process of making becomes a small attempt to interrogate the girls' indoctrinated inadequacy as social participants and their ineligibility to critique educational, domestic and political systems in which they must operate. The dolls are *their* dolls, fragments of themselves to love, play with, give away, or sell.

Conclusion

This article highlights the possibilities of meaning that can be uncovered by an exploration of the social and personal significance of children's dolls. Deliberate remembering enables the strand of connection between the adult world and that of the child to be maintained. In the absence of this tether, an engaged understanding of current childhood culture becomes less likely. Working directly with dolls as creative productions is an obvious extension that calls for further examination. Whether in the art classroom or outside the school environment, the DIY doll presents the potential for girls to participate in the construction of girlhood identities. Such creative acts do not eradicate vulnerability but they do offer a way of navigating the confines of social constructs. The handmade doll can operate both as a conduit to external realities of young girls and a catalyst to change in their sense of self. In the face of tumultuous circumstances, making a doll can mean literally and figuratively taking something into one's own hands regardless of how small those hands are or how small the act of affirmation.

CR ─────────────────────────────────────

Dr. April Mandrona is an Assistant Professor and the Director of Art Education at NSCAD University. She received a PhD in Art Education from Concordia University and was a SSHRC postdoctoral fellow at McGill University. Mandrona's current SSHRC-funded research supports children with refugee experience in making picture books that reflect their perspectives and creativity. Mandrona has published on rurality, young people's visual culture, art education, ethics, and participatory research. Recent co-edited volumes include *Visual Encounters in the Study of Rural Childhoods* (Rutgers, 2018), *Our Rural Selves: Memory, Place, and the Visual in Canadian Rural Childhoods* (MQUP, 2019), and *Ethical Practice in Participatory Visual Research with Girls* (Berghahn, In Press).

───────────────────────────────────── RO

Acknowledgments

I would like to acknowledge Dr Claudia Mitchell whose editorial and conceptual input contributed greatly to this paper, and whose enthusiasm, support and insight has inspired much of my doctoral work.

References

Attfield, Judy. 1996. "Barbie and Action Man: Adult Toys for Girls and Boys, 1959–1993." Pp. 80–89 in *The Gendered Object,* ed. P. Kirkham. New York: Manchester University Press.

Attfield, Judy. 2000. *Wild Things: The Material Culture of Everyday Life.* New York: Berg.

Brown, Dona. 2011. *Back to the Land: The Enduring Dream of Self-sufficiency in Modern America.* Madison, WI: University of Wisconsin Press.

Butler, Judith. 2004. *Undoing Gender.* New York: Routledge.

Carrington, Victoria. 2003. "'I'm in a Bad Mood. Let's Go Shopping': Interactive Dolls, Consumer Culture and a 'Glocalized' Model of Literacy." *Journal of Early Childhood Literacy* 3, no. 1: 83–98.

Charles, Claire. 2010. "Competing Hetero-Femininities: Young Women, Sexualities and 'Girl Power' at School". *International Journal of Qualitative Studies in Education* 23, no. 1: 33–47.

Der Ananian, Greg. 2005. *Bazaar Bizarre: Not Your Granny's Crafts.* New York: Viking Studio.

Eisenhauer, Jennifer. 2004. "Mythic Figures and Lived Identities: Locating the 'Girl' in Feminist Discourse". Pp. 79–90 in *All About the Girl: Culture, Power and Identity,* ed. A. Harris. New York: Routledge.

Forman-Brunell, Miriam. 2009. "Barbie in 'Life': The Life of Barbie." *Journal of the History of Childhood & Youth* 2, no. 3: 303–311.

Formanek-Brunell, Miriam. 1993. *Made to Play House: Dolls and the Commercialization of American Girlhood, 1830–1930*. New Haven, CT: Yale University Press.

Fraser, Nancy. 2009. "Feminism, Capitalism and the Cunning of History." *New Left Review* 56: 97–117.

Gaitskell, Deborah. 1999. "Beyond 'Devout Domesticity': Five Female Mission Strategies in South Africa, 1907–1960." *Transformation* 16: 127–135.

Harris, Anita. 2004. *All About the Girl: Culture, Power, and Identity*. New York: Routledge.

HubPages. 2010. "Liv Fashion Dolls." <http://whitney05.hubpages.com/hub/Liv-Fashion-Dolls> (accessed 15 May 2011).

Jenkins, Henry. 2009. *Confronting the Challenges of Participatory Culture: Media Education for the 21st Century*. Cambridge: MIT Press.

Kuhn, Annette. 1995. *Family Secrets: Acts of Memory and Imagination*. New York: Verso.

Kuhn, Annette. 2010. "Memory Texts and Memory Work: Performances of Memory in and with Visual Media." *Memory Studies* 3, no. 4: 298–313.

Laurel, Alicia B. 1970. *Living on the Earth*. Berkeley, CA: The Book Works.

Miller, Jane. 1995. "Trick or Treat? The Autobiography of the Question." *English Quarterly* 27, no. 3: 22–26.

Mitchell, Claudia. 2010. "Researching Things, Objects and Gendered Consumption in Childhood Studies." Pp. 94–112 in *Childhood and Consumer Culture*, eds. D. Buckingham and V. Tinstad. New York: St. Martin's Press.

Mitchell, Claudia, and Jacqueline Reid-Walsh. 2002. *Researching Children's Popular Culture: The Cultural Spaces of Childhood*. New York: Routledge.

National Department of Health South Africa. 2011. *National Antenatal Sentinel HIV and Syphilis Prevalence Survey*. Pretoria: National Department of Health.

Peers, Juliet. 2004. *The Fashion Doll: From Bébé Jumeau to Barbie*. New York: Berg.

Poletti, Anna. 2008. *Intimate Ephemera: Reading Young Lives in Australian Zine Culture*. Melbourne: Melbourne University Press.

Ramjee, Gita, Handan Wand, Claire Whitaker, Sheena McCormack, Nancy Padian, Cliff Kelly, and Andrew Nunn. 2011. "HIV Incidence Among Non-Pregnant Women Living in Selected Rural, Semi-Rural and Urban Areas in Kwazulu-Natal, South Africa." *AIDS and Behavior*. doi: 10.1007/s10461-011-0043-7

Rowbotham, Sheila. 2008. "Arts, Crafts & Socialism." *History Today* 59, no. 2: 44–50.

Smith, Rochelle. 2010. "Antislick to Postslick: DIY Books and Youth Culture Then and Now." *The Journal of American Culture* 33, no. 3: 207–216.

Spigel, Lynn. 2001. *Welcome to the Dreamhouse: Popular Media and Postwar Suburbs*. Durham, NC: Duke University Press.

Stewart, Susan. 1984. *On Longing: Narratives of the Miniature, the Gigantic, the Souvenir, the Collection*. Baltimore: John Hopkins University Press.

Vincentelli, Moira. 2003. *Women Potters: Transforming Traditions*. New Brunswick, NJ: Rutgers.

Chapter 6

An Afternoon of Productive Play with Problematic Dolls
The Importance of Foregrounding Children's Voices in Research

Rebecca C. Hains

ॐ

Introduction

Since their introduction in 2001, Bratz dolls have been popular with pre-teen girls for their trendy hip-hop style, edgy fashion sensibility, and racial diversity. Their manufacturer, MGA Entertainment, markets Bratz to girls as young as preschool age and sets a reasonable price point of roughly $8 to $15 per doll. The original four dolls—Cloe, Jade, Sasha, and Jasmin—and their friends have appeared in many fashionable variations, including Bratz Girlz Really Rock band, Bratz Masquerade dolls featuring makeup for their young owners, "super-sparkly"

Bratz All Glammed Up dolls with stylable "memory hair," and Bratz Genie Magic dolls who "express[ed] their flair for Far East fashion, and far-out colors." MGA also produced brand extensions such as Baby Bratz, Bratz Kidz, Bratz Boyz, and Bratz Familiez. All Bratz dolls shared a "passion for fashion,"[1] the brand's organizing principle; MGA positioned Bratz as having the best clothing and style of any fashion doll. Despite the extreme tightness of some of their clothing, the dolls are easy to dress because their feet detach. Related products such as the Bratz magazine encouraged girls to imagine wearing Bratz fashions, furthering their brand identification.

Bratz dolls' rise to commercial dominance—which included global sales of $2 billion by 2005, accompanied by additional Bratz media properties and licensed goods—ousted Barbie from its seemingly unstoppable 50-year-long reign. Bratz significantly reduced Barbie's U.S. sales and outsold Barbie two to one in the U.K. Mattel responded by releasing "My Scene Barbie" dolls, whose aesthetic approximated that of the Bratz, and sued MGA for allegedly stealing Mattel's designs and trade secrets. Drawn-out legal battles hurt the Bratz brand, stopping production for two years when the courts reassigned the Bratz copyright to Mattel. In 2011, the courts overturned this ruling, and MGA won a countersuit against Mattel for stealing MGA's trade secrets (Riley 2011; Kavilanz 2011). New toys such as Bratz Party dolls are now available for purchase; promotional copy explains: "Bratz are celebrating 10 years of being the life of the party. They always bring their sassy spirit, signature style, and a whole lotta' attitude. When you're a Bratz, they're [sic] sooo much to celebrate."

While industry watchers may consider the Mattel v. MGA outcome the triumph of an upstart business against a deep-pocketed international behemoth, not everyone celebrates MGA's vindication. Bratz have had many critics; most have argued the dolls over-emphasize appearance and are too sexy for young girls. (Even though Barbie and her unrealistic curves were the subject of much feminist critique, Mattel responded by producing career-oriented Barbies—astronauts, teachers, and so on, helping girls dream about many possible future roles.) The underlying cause for concern is an awareness of dolls' ongoing roles in the socialization of girls. For example, baby dolls have been understood to teach girls about their expected future roles as wives and mothers. Wertheimer (2006) has argued that in the age of Barbie and Bratz, "doll play remains a key tool in helping girls learn the gendered roles and expectations of their cultures and societies" (218)—but rather than emphasizing the maternal care an infant requires, fashion dolls emphasize girls' future roles as consumers of the various products and services required to produce normative femininity: hairstyle, makeup, clothes, and accessories—ranging from jewelry to flashy cars—are critically important.

A broader trend has compounded critics' concerns about Bratz: the sexualization of girls. In the same decade as the ascent of Bratz to global popularity, psychologists, educators, media studies scholars, and others decried popular culture texts and products for encouraging ever-younger girls to pursue age-inappropriate appearances and behaviors. Critics argued that young girls are developmentally unable to comprehend the sexual implications of the products and styles they are asked to embrace, with psychologically detrimental consequences (American Psychological Association 2007). In this vein, scholars and activists have repeatedly cited Bratz as exemplars of the sexualized mainstream products targeting girls. For example:

- The APA Task Force on the Sexualization of Girls singled out Bratz for "dress[ing] in sexualized clothing such as miniskirts, fishnet stockings, and feather boas" (APA 2007: para. 9).
- In *The Lolita Effect: The Media Sexualization of Young Girls and What We Can Do About It,* Durham (2008) recalls a young girl who, dressed for Halloween as a Bratz doll, reminded her of "a child prostitute I had seen in Cambodia" (21).
- In *Packaging Girlhood: Rescuing Our Daughters From Marketers' Schemes,* Lamb and Brown (2006) concluded that Bratz teach girls to "practice being sex objects" (219).

Meanwhile, scholars writing cultural studies analyses of Bratz dolls could not escape the brands' bold pattern of sexualization. In McAllister's (2007) essay "'Girls with a Passion for Fashion': The Bratz Brand as Integrated Spectacular Consumption," which explored the brand's promotion of a consumerist-oriented lifestyle, he noted that the Bratz and their skimpy, provocative clothes are "sexualized and therefore sold as defiantly adult-oriented fashion" to children—who are further encouraged to purchase other Bratz products, such as electronics and clothing, "to achieve a similar empowering sexuality/maturity" (251).

Like scholars, critics writing for the popular media have expressed many concerns about Bratz and sexualization. For example, *The New Yorker* pithily observed, "[Bratz] look like pole dancers on their way to work at a gentlemen's club" (Talbott 2006); the *Boston Globe* said the dolls were "asking for trouble" (Meltz 2003); and the *New York Times* suggested that Bratz "look as though they might be at home on any street corner where prostitutes ply their trade" (LaFerla 2003).

Scholars have also raised concerns about the problematic use of race in the Bratz brand. Guerrero (2009) argued that the brand exploits racial difference as something "hip," making "otherness" the equivalent to a fashion accessory (189–190). Orr (2009) argues that the sexiness inherent in Bratz dolls, which "average several shades darker than Barbie," is no coincidence: "The stereotypes of the overly sexualized woman of color are well-established. In the case of the Bratz dolls, their colour stands as one more signifier for sexy" (24). Valdivia (2011) critiques Bratz as looking ambiguously Latina, hybridizing a Latina identity in such a subtle way "that it can be harnessed to represent any, all, or no difference" (98–99). Meanwhile, McAllister (2007) documents how MGA deliberately employed strategic ambiguity in the dolls' racial identities, making it impossible to tell with certainty the ethnic identity of the majority of Bratz dolls. He quoted one MGA executive as "crassly" describing the global advantages of this strategy: "We don't even market them as belonging to a particular race. We have little girls in South America who think Sasha is South African, girls in Samoa who things [sic] she is Samoan and girls in the United States who think she is from Harlem" (quoted in McAllister 2007: 248). McAllister concluded that from a marketing perspective, the Bratz dolls' racial diversity functions in service to their hyperfeminine sexualization. The brand's racial diversity is meant to encourage as many girls as possible to identify with the Bratz look and engage in the Bratz lifestyle.

Expanding the Conversation: Girls and their Bratz Dolls

In myriad conversations about the trouble with Bratz, one voice has been missing: that of young girls. What have girls thought of Bratz, and how have they negotiated the ideologies embedded within Bratz dolls during their play? Guerrero (2009) noted that because of their racial diversity,

Bratz dolls had "oppositional potential" (194), but how girls employed this potential was beyond the scope of her essay. Likewise, McAllister (2007) noted that the premise of integrated spectacular consumption assumes—problematically—a passive audience, and mentioned that some girls might benefit from more positive Bratz themes, but exploring this was beyond the scope of his essay, as well. In this manner, scholarly analyses of Bratz have focused on products without input from girls.

The lack of scholarship on Bratz dolls' reception reflects a broader pattern in the field of girlhood studies: scholars often criticize popular culture targeting girls without attending to real girls' voices, a pattern scholars as Kearney (2011) have criticized, calling for more research *with* girls. To address this gap in the girlhood studies literature, I conducted fieldwork about girls' media culture with more than thirty preadolescent girls, most between the ages of 8 and 10 years. I sought to learn about the roles of girl power television in girls' lives and to understand how girls received the programs' girl power messages (Hains 2012). During this research, Bratz dolls were at the height of their popularity, and although Bratz were not the focus of my study, it was impossible to escape their prevalence in my participants' lives. Most girls in my study owned many Bratz dolls—in some cases, enough to fill entire bins. When the *Bratz* computer-animated television series debuted in late 2005, it was immediately popular among my participants.

At the same time, I was aware of concerns regarding Bratz dolls and their sexualization, so I attended to the girls' interest in Bratz. I recorded several conversations—some relatively brief—about Bratz and other dolls. These culminated in a lengthy show-and-tell playtime in which a group of African-American girls demonstrated how they sometimes played with their Bratz dolls. In this article, I offer a brief case study of Bratz dolls' reception among that group of African-American girls. I found that despite the problematic aspects of Bratz dolls, these girls created productive avenues for Bratz play, actively making meanings that conflicted with the producers' intentions for the dolls. This unexpected finding does not necessarily mitigate the negative aspects of the Bratz brand or exonerate its marketers for promoting a sexual object position among young girls. It offers, however, a more multifaceted perspective of the actual uses of Bratz among girls, with insights into the methodological limitations of analyzing children's popular and material culture as texts.

Methodology

From 2005 to 2006, I held regular meetings with three groups of girls to discuss girl power and girls' media culture. Our meetings were held in adjacent towns in a major urban area of the east coast of the United States. The groups were as follows:

1. At the Nonprofit Aftercare Program: 13 African-American girls and one Caucasian girl.
2. At the Suburban Elementary Aftercare Program: 9 Caucasian girls and one African-American girl.
3. At the Township Public Library: 4 African-American girls, 6 Caucasian girls and one Indian-American girl.

Using book clubs as a model. I operated each group as a video club: we watched videos together and then discussed them. As detailed in my book, *Growing Up With Girl Power* (Hains 2012), we primarily screened television cartoons featuring girl heroes, such as *The Powerpuff Girls, Kim Possible,* and *Totally Spies,* as I sought to learn about girl power media's roles in the girls' everyday lives.

Because of the meandering nature of our conversations and the time I spent with them outside our video group—at lunch recess, on the playground, and during library period—I also observed patterns such as how girls of varying racial and socioeconomic backgrounds used consumption to define their identities. They had differing resources at their disposal, which translated to different products, for example, which dolls they favored. During my study, the participants mentioned American Girl dolls and Bratz dolls most frequently, but their popularity varied among the groups of girls.

Among the Caucasian girls in my study, who were predominantly middle class, American Girl dolls were popular; most owned more than one. These expensive, upscale dolls look similar to fine classic porcelain dolls and cost over $100 each. Each doll is bundled with a book situating her in a specific historical era, reflected in the doll's period clothing and accessories (most sold separately at high price points). These historic backstories appeal to middle-class parents, as they suggest the dolls are educational in nature and worth the high price. The stories appeal to girls, as well. My informants could speak eloquently about which American Girl they wanted to be like and the era to which their doll belonged. The dolls' selling conditions further justify their cost: their sale via catalog and in upscale stores reinforces the brand's luxury/high-quality ethos.

Meanwhile, most African-American participants, many in the lower-middle socioeconomic class, lacked access to American Girl dolls. They longed for them anyway, and in some cases, their families did their best to provide affordable substitutes. For example, one girl shared a por-celain doll that her father had purchased, telling her that it was "ten times more expensive than an American Girl doll." She seemed proud to own such a special toy. However, I have seen similar dolls for $15 to $25, less than a quarter of the cost of an American Girl doll.

While American Girl dolls were available only to girls whose fami-lies had the economic means to afford them, nearly all participants played with Bratz, available for as little as $8. Their popularity cut across race and socioeconomic class. All Bratz owners reported playing with their dolls as expected, styling their hair and dressing them up. Many also wished they could dress like the dolls, bringing to mind con-cerns that Bratz encourage girls to dress in sexually provocative clothing despite being too young to understand what sexy means. As an example of this, one seven-year-old Caucasian girl in my study commented to her eight-year-old sister that when girls wear bras, they look "hotter." When I asked her what that meant, she replied, "It kinda means, like, hot means, like, you're cute"—an innocent definition with which most adults would disagree.

Despite Bratz dolls' general popularity, the Caucasian girls who owned American Girl dolls seemed to cherish them more than their Bratz, perhaps because their cost and comparative scarcity made them dearer. They were eager to show me their American Girls dolls, perhaps because they felt they were special. In contrast, for most of the African-American girls in my study, Bratz were their go-to dolls. I believe this was partly because their economic realities meant they lacked some of the nicer (costlier, middle-class-oriented) choices that other girls in my study enjoyed. Significantly, however, the African-American girls I interviewed at Nonprofit Aftercare played with Bratz in a way that I believe the Caucasian girls did not: although Bratz wear contemporary fashions and are unavailable in historical dress, some African-American participants demonstrated that they used the racial diversity of Bratz to negotiate issues concerned with race and U.S. history. While playing in this way, they appeared to ignore the dolls' sexy clothing, focusing instead on skin tone variations as they wove an array of stories. It would appear that these girls bracketed or ignored the dolls' sexualized aspects as they focused more selectively upon the aspects that seem to have most preoccupied (and possibly empowered) them—namely, that some of dolls had skin tones like their own.

In the rest of this article, I explore how the African-American girls in my study used Bratz doll play to explore race and history. In so doing, I present a perspective different from that of prior Bratz scholarship and offer methodological considerations for those interested in material culture products' influence upon children. Note that my aim is not to contradict previous scholarship about Bratz; I agree the sexiness imposed on children by Bratz dolls is significantly problematic. Bratz and other sexy products and texts warrant concern from scholars, parents, activists, and educators alike. However, by approaching the question of Bratz dolls' role in girls' lives from a different methodological vantage point, I witnessed that for at least some girls, Bratz play is not solely focused on the dolls' sexualized characteristics. I argue that Bratz dolls' racial diversity provided the African-American girls in my study with an avenue to explore race, racism, and U.S. history.

The Salience of Race in Bratz Doll Play

Critics have long regarded the whiteness of dolls, whether baby dolls or fashion dolls, as a problem for children of color who play with dolls. According to Ann duCille's (1996) *Skin Trade,* dolls and other toys are understood as "assist[ing] children in the process of becoming, in the task of defining themselves in relation to the world around them" (17). In the U.S., the blonde-haired, blue-eyed beauty ideal embodied by Barbie was the most readily available fashion doll for girls for decades; and in the baby doll market, it was easier to find light-skinned, blue-eyed baby dolls than those with any other physical characteristics. (During my girlhood in the 1970s and 1980s, I remember feeling badly that there were so few Caucasian dolls with brown hair and brown eyes, like me.) Considering the ramifications of this for girls of color, duCille (1994) asks: "What does it mean ... when little girls are given dolls that in no way resemble them?" (46). Scholars have suggested that when they are surrounded by white dolls in a culture that idealizes whiteness, young girls may surrender and accept this as the norm, and fantasize themselves as being more like their white dolls or other white heroes (see duCille 1996; Guerrero 2009). From her position as an African-American woman who was born a decade before Barbie, duCille (2006) has argued convincingly that when a black child grows up in such a context, "dreaming white is the natural response to what the child sees and does not see in society's looking glass" (13).

Because my African-American participants grew up alongside Bratz, they had a small advantage over previous generations—greater diversity in doll selection. Despite Bratz dolls' flaws, their skin tones ranged from very light to very dark, more like real girls'. At the same time, these participants were also sensitive to the racialization of other dolls. Rhea[2] (aged 9) explained, "For the black Barbie dolls, they give 'em, like, orange and everything before the white, and [for the white] one, they give her, like, pink and blue or something. A lot of black people hate orange!" Rhea's observation brings to mind duCille's (1994) argument that many multicultural Barbies from the 1980s were basically white Barbies, "modified only by a dash of color [darker skin] and a change of costume" (51): African-American girls like Rhea who could see through this "costume" change had a problem with it. They wanted fashionably dressed dolls, not dolls swathed in unpopular colors like orange. Madison (aged 9) agreed with Rhea's assessment, explaining how these politics informed her shopping choices: "I buy Bratz dolls because all of them—all the Bratz dolls are treated right." How might she have understood Bratz dolls to be "treated right"? Arguably, Madison could see that Bratz of various skin tones were treated as individuals, with distinct personalities and equally fashionable styles. Unlike the Barbie line, the darker-hued Bratz dolls were not offered as costumed, "dye-dipped" versions of their iconic blonde sister (duCille 1994: 49). While Barbie remained in center stage as the *real* Barbie even after Mattel began producing non-white Barbies (Rand 1998), all Bratz shared the stage in advertisements. The Bratz were a peer group, a diverse group of friends—whereas the Barbies seemed presented in a hierarchical fashion, with white Barbie at the top.

Scholars have noted that a Bratz doll's most salient signifier of race is her skin tone, for other features of Bratz scarcely vary. Valdivia (2011) argues that all Bratz dolls' faces look ambiguously Latina (98), for no matter their skin tones, they all have stereotypically Latina facial characteristics: full lips, wide-set almond-shaped eyes, and straight hair. The vague Latinadad of all Bratz dolls offered a new variation on the construction of multicultural Barbies.

Within this context of changing racial representations in the fashion doll industry, the girls' Bratz doll play occurred. After spending many months meeting regularly with three groups of girls in a semi-structured fashion, with room for much variance between the three groups, I observed one group's play with Bratz dolls in a "show and tell" session. This particular group had asked if I would bring them a *Bratz* television episode to watch during our video club time. I had some unspoken reservations about the brand, but I suggested that if they would bring their Bratz dolls to school to share with me, we could screen a *Bratz* episode together afterwards.

During group meetings, I normally set up a camcorder in an unobtrusive location and recorded our conversations. On special occasions, however, in which we were doing something more than discussing a video we had screened—for example, examining magazines, or discussing a topic of an individual girls' choosing, led by that girl—the girls recorded our meetings from their own perspectives. The Bratz show-and-tell afternoon was such an occasion: handing them the camcorder, I gave them as much control as possible over the direction of our meeting and conversation. During this girl-led and girl-recorded discussion, I expressed interest and asked the occasional clarifying question, but I tried to stay out of their way.

When I handed the girls my camcorder, I made a simple request: that they give the camera a tour, as it were, of their dolls. They described each Bratz doll in succession. For example, Desirée (aged 9) gave voice to Sasha, a dark-skinned doll, as saying, "I'm the cutest one of the Bratz"; then, Zayonna (aged 10) made Cameron—a light-skinned doll, and the only male Bratz they had that day—kiss Felicia, the darkest-skin doll, repeatedly. Their dramatic make-out session prompted Desirée to nudge Zayonna and say, "OK, I don't wanna see that!"

During this beginning part of our session together, the girls conversed about the dolls' fashions in ways that would alarm anyone familiar with the literature on girls' sexualization, for they expressed their wishes to dress like the Bratz dolls and emulate them. Desirée offered,

"When I think of the Bratz, it's because they're so cool because I like their clothes. And their hair is so cool because you can do it and stuff, and give them makeovers. And, I like her skirt. It's real fashionable. They have bracelets. And it's so cool because you can take off their feet to take off the shoes."

Soon after this, however, their conversation took an unpredictable turn as the girls began using the dolls to act out race relations at their predominantly black schools, and then to explore their understandings of the U.S. history of slavery and the Underground Railroad.

Desirée prompted this turn in their conversation when she announced, "I'm gonna give you an interview [about] how people ... treat each other in real life as Caucasians (holding up Cloe) and African-Americans (holding up Sasha)." In this scenario, she created a school setting in which African-Americans were the majority and other races were the minority—reflecting her school's composition. In a narrative based upon her lunchroom experiences, Desirée used Bratz to tell a story in which a white doll approached two black dolls seated together during lunch, saying that she wanted to sit with them. One black doll spoke welcomingly to the white doll, but her friend balked; this hurt the white doll's feelings. Desirée explained, "That's how ... that's how people ... that's how my friend got offended at my other friend."

Desiree's second scenario served as a corrective to the first; she shared her vision for greater social inclusively. Desirée explained, "If she (referencing one of her dolls) walked up to the first [doll] and said, 'Why are you sitting next to that white person?' instead of just sitting there, she could stand up and say, 'Because I want to. Because she's my friend. Not like you. That's a rude thing to say.'" She added that if the black doll insulted the white friend, she could also say, "That's not cool. That's offending her."

Desirée's stories offered an intriguing snapshot of girls' Bratz play. She did not seem to be mimicking a television narrative; instead, she was illustrating events that had transpired in her own life. Although this may or may not have been a snapshot of her usual Bratz play, it still offers some insights: despite the dolls' problematic attributes, Desirée's stories suggested that girls could appropriate the dolls in order to act out scenarios of relevance to their everyday lives, abetted by the dolls' variations in skin tones. This snapshot came to life vividly after Madison (aged 9) requested a turn to do her own "show." Following

Desirée's lead, Madison also offered a story on race relations—detailing "how White people treat Black people, and how Black people treat White people, back then." The story she told was more detailed and it required her friends' help. As a group, the girls therefore used the Bratz dolls to enact their understandings of U.S. slavery's history and the Underground Railroad's role in bringing slaves to freedom. This collaborative story, which unfolded over more than ten minutes, took no preparation; the girls followed Madison's lead with ease. As they developed their story, the girls acted as *bricoleurs,* drawing upon classroom lessons and mainstream media content.

The girls began by dismissing the visual characteristics of the Bratz that have been a source of critics' concerns: their clothing.

> Madison: OK. These are slaves, and …
>
> Zayonna: They're some *cute* slaves. Look at their clothes! (She laughs)
>
> Interviewer: (laughing with Zayonna) They're really well-dressed slaves.
>
> Madison: Pretend they have raggedy clothes.
>
> Desirée: *Raggedy* clothes.

Thus, while Bratz dolls and their marketing may influence girls to identify as sexual objects, the dolls' racial diversity appeared to have enabled these girls to create new scripts not intended by the manufacturer for their dolls. The dolls' clothing and accessories encode the ideas and values of American-style consumerism, but these girls' imaginations seemed to have been influenced by the dolls' variable skin tones, even in the absence of any other true forms of variation. This variance arguably disrupted the standardized narrative of Bratz as exclusively fashion-oriented.

With the girls following Madison's directive to overlook the dolls' trendy clothing (pretending they had "raggedy clothes"), their collaborative play established several characters along the way. The characters were as follows:

- Two black dolls (Sasha and one of unknown name): Slaves
- A white female Bratz doll (Cloe): Cruel slave owner
- One white male Bratz doll (Cameron): White person who informed the slaves about the Underground Railroad; later reimagined as Cloe's husband who secretly opposed slavery

- A white baby Bratz doll (name unknown): The person the slaves met at the first stop on the Underground Railroad; later, stripped of her detachable ponytail to play a homeowner at another stop of the Underground Railroad.

Madison started her story by portraying a slave owner with the white Cloe doll, bossing her terrified slaves around menacingly. Bailey (aged 10) and Desirée played the slaves, while Madison additionally played Cameron, the white boy Bratz doll. They began as follows:

Madison/Cloe: (speaking sharply to the Black dolls) Get to work!

Bailey/Black Dolls: (in fear) No! (The dolls had been lying down; they now stand bolt upright. They begin jumping up and down.)

Madison/Cloe: (menacingly) Hurry up. Stop playin' around! (The Black dolls had been jumping; they jumped faster.)

Madison: (narrating) Some people … some White people that they didn't even notice tried to help them.

Madison/Cameron: (whispering to the black dolls) Stop doing the work. Stop doing the work! You can go to the Underground Railroad.

Bailey: (quietly) With Harriet Tubman.

Zayonna: (loudly, directly into the camera) With Harriet Tubman.

Madison/Cameron: Harriet Tubman. She's at the Underground Railroad. She's trying to save people. Go tomorrow! Tomorrow will be … tomorrow will be …

Desirée/Sasha: (whispering) Tomorrow morning at dawn.

Madison/Cameron: No, tomorrow *night*. Because then … because it's frozen …

Unknown: In the rivers we get a head start.

Madison/Cameron: (whispering) OK.

As this exchange illustrates, as the girls' narrative proceeded, they built upon one another's contributions and, when it came to factual historical content, corrected each other freely. Likewise, when the girls declared night had fallen, they recalled the signals of the Underground Railroad together:

Bailey: When the first crow calls, (singing) "Follow the drinking gourd."

Desirée/Sasha: (whispering to the black dolls) We have to hurry up and go. Let's go. (The dolls exit, crossing the table.) OK, here's our first stop.

We have to ask somebody how to get to ... how to get to the next stop. Who you gonna ask? Her!

Bailey: Pretend she's a, you know ...

Rebecca: Pretend she's a what?

Bailey: One of the station people.

Madison/Baby Bratz Doll: I'm sorry I'm a midget (everyone laughs), but I live in this house. I will keep you safe, and I will tell you the next house to go to. You keep on going and going until you see front leg, pat leg.

Rebecca: (softly) Until you see what?

Madison: Front leg, pat leg.

Zayonna: (emphatically) *Peg*. (The girls were referring to "Left foot, peg foot," a sign on the Underground Railroad trail said to have been left by a one-legged Railroad organizer known as Peg Leg Joe.)

Madison/Baby Bratz Doll: And sing that "Follow the Drinking Gourd" (in which the line "Left foot, peg foot, goin' on" appears in the second verse).

At this point, with the slave dolls on their road to freedom, all the girls joined Bailey in singing a stanza from the song "Follow the Drinking Gourd," a folksong believed to have helped runaway slaves follow the North Star to freedom. I asked how the girls knew this song, and they explained that they had learned the song in music class at school.

Madison, playing the Cloe doll, then confronted the baby Bratz doll, still acting as an Underground Railroad conductor, about her missing slaves. Cloe asked the baby Bratz, "Have you seen any *slaaaaves*?" When the baby Bratz said no, Cloe insisted upon looking through her house and—suddenly voiced by Zayonna—became angry, shouting, "Don't lie to me, woman." As Madison had Cloe search the attic of the baby Bratz doll's house, she obsessively hunted from side to side and behind imagined boxes without success.

Madison/Cloe: ("upstairs" in the TV cart, addressing the baby Bratz doll): Your attic is humongous! A *lot* of slaves could be here. *Anywhere*. Behind those boxes! (She scoots suddenly across the TV to look.) No.... (quickly) Behind *there*! (She scoots along the side of the TV.) No.... (The doll comes back downstairs to the table to the other White dolls.) If you find one, contact me at 555-1234.

Zayonna: That's your phone number, Madison! You know that? (Laughter)

After the girls' laughter subsided, I asked where the slaves were. Desirée had been playing with a different Bratz doll during Madison's slave hunting and seemed momentarily lost, but she recovered quickly. Then the girls had the runaway slave dolls "cross the frozen water" to freedom. When Desirée said, "They finally made it to the South," Zayonna helped again with the historical facts, asking, "You mean North?" Desirée agreed, repeating, "North." Desirée then began a conversation between the two runaway slave dolls—the first time the girls had given either of them a voice thus far—presenting them as sisters. She voiced one as saying to the other, "What about all the other slaves and your husband back there? Don't you want to go and get 'em?" Her sister replied, "Yes, I do love my John." The first doll replied, "OK, let's go."

Recognizing the line "I do love my John" as dialogue from a television program that I had recently begun watching because these girls enjoyed it so much, I asked, "Isn't that a line from *Sister, Sister?*" The girls began laughing, and a chuckling Desirée explained, "I saw it last night." (The episode was about the Underground Railroad and featured a fictitious Harriet Tubman.) In this way, the girls' current media consumption informed both their doll play and their understanding of U.S. history; they wove these disparate threads together into their *bricolage* of Bratz doll play.

Abruptly, Madison began driving the narrative again, portraying Cloe as persistently continuing to hunt her runaway slaves. Madison/Cloe cried, "I need my slaves! I'll hunt them down with doggies if I have to!" But then Madison portrayed the boy Bratz doll, Cameron, as Cloe's husband, and explained that he secretly disagreed with slavery. Therefore, he tried to stop her, but she insisted, "No. I can *feel* them." Madison then explained, "Back then, they would do anything to get their slaves. (In an ominous voice) *Anything!* (Musing) I don't know if they would sell their house," she added, speculating as to whether home ownership was more or less important to slave owners than maintaining possession of their slaves. And on that note, the girls' portrayal of the Underground Railroad with Bratz dolls concluded.

Discussion

Although the girls' intriguing Bratz play session lasted for just one afternoon, it confirmed several established understandings. Play "offers a key site to begin negotiating certain of the fears and tensions intrinsic to one's cultural and social environment" (Wertheimer 2006: 219), and the girls' doll play certainly seemed to be accomplishing work of this nature. Wondering whether they usually played with their Bratz dolls in ways that ignored the dolls' intended fashion play, I inquired about this; in response, the girls discussed their play habits among themselves, agreeing that they did sometimes, but not *all* the time. After I walked away to speak with Madison in another part of the room, Desirée, still controlling the camera, asked Zayonna if she had ever played "slaves" before. Zayonna replied in the affirmative and offered an example:

> One time I put ... I was playing with Sasha and Felicia and the rest of her family. She has ... (pauses to count) ...five younger sisters. So, um, they were all showed to be different people. Like, the rest of the Bratz dolls were, like, (hesitates, then says a little more softly) *Caucasian*. So (speaking in full voice again), I made one of the ladies, pretend that they were, um, slaves, [and] they made Sasha's mom one of the workers. And Sasha's mom eventually died because she didn't have any food. She was hot and she didn't bathe, and she was really nasty.

It would appear that for these girls, the Bratz dolls' racial diversity afforded them the opportunity to explore privately the dark history of racism and slavery in the United States, as well as the modern race relations they were attempting to negotiate in school (as in Desiree's lunchroom stories). A number of other related themes that emerged included:

- Problems between African-Americans and Caucasians, ranging from modern social tensions to historic violence and enslavement;
- An awareness of the viciousness of some white people who were slave owners, with Cloe—the "whitest" Bratz doll, with the lightest hair—playing the cruelest character;
- A desire to explore solutions to these problems;
- A recognition that, historically, white people disagreed with one another regarding the morality of slavery;

- A demonstration of their awareness of the important roles played by specific blacks (Harriet Tubman, Peg Leg Joe) in the fight to abolish slavery; and
- The ability to draw freely upon a range of knowledge during play, including history learned in school, songs from music class, and media content as they played with Bratz.

In generating stories with these characteristics, the girls engaged in important work, abetted by their ability to ignore the intended purposes of Bratz: they could ignore the dolls' shiny, fashionable clothes and pretend they had "raggedy clothes." The stories of slavery they imagined during our time together—and during their reported private play at home—grappled with far darker elements of U.S. history than does any American Girl doll's backstory. As the girls knew that prejudice, stereotyping, and discrimination were ongoing issues in the world around them, this play seems to have been personally and collectively useful as they developed and explored their identities as pre-teen African-American girls, with everything culturally encompassed by that identity.

Methodologically, these findings were made possible by at least two considerations. The first concerns my ongoing relationship with the girls. Meeting twice weekly for several months, we developed relationships in which the girls felt comfortable taking risks around me. Before launching into her narrative of slavery with the Bratz dolls, Madison took a deep breath and told me, "I trust you." In reviewing our videotape and transcript, nothing specific appears to have prompted this declaration. However, it seems to indicate that for at least a moment, she thought twice about sharing this story with me. Perhaps she briefly wondered if the story would offend me because I am Caucasian, or perhaps she thought that as an adult, I might be judgmental, or both—or something else entirely. In any case, it is unclear whether someone of similar background to me (a Caucasian female) could enter a group of African-American pre-teen girls and immediately witness their play in such honest ways. Indeed, reviewing the video and its transcript, it seems that Zayonna—who had joined the group after the others, and did not have as long-term a relationship with me as did her friends—hesitated to bring up the way she engaged in slave play at home and to use the word "Caucasian" in front of me. She waited until I was out of earshot to tell Desirée, who was handling the video camera, directly.

I had previously reassured the other girls that I would not be offended if they used terms like "Caucasian," "little white girls," and so on in reference to white people; somewhere along the way, they had been taught, either explicitly or implicitly, that it was rude to do so, and for the sake of our conversations, I wanted them to know I disagreed with that perspective. Madison's expression of trust and Zayonna's apparent reservation reinforce my belief that in conducting research with children, ethnographic approaches, though time consuming, are of great value. They can yield more interesting and unexpected data than briefer, more structured approaches.

The second consideration is the girls' power to shape the course of field research. If I had held the video camera and simply asked questions about the Bratz dolls, I might never have learned that they played with their dolls to negotiate issues of race, racism, and history. Because I approached my research with a desire to be as non-hierarchical as possible—making myself what is known as a near peer and distancing myself as much as possible from a position of authority—I believe the girls felt more control over the narrative they were creating. Their afternoon of Bratz play was a fruitful example of the usefulness of encouraging the girls to take the lead: holding the camera empowered the girls to state, with directorial intention, what stories they were going to tell, and to choose who and what they would show as their narratives unfolded.

In conclusion, children's use of pop culture—as evidenced by the African-American girls' play with Bratz dolls—is probably more complex than we, as adults, might conclude from simplistic impressions of popular media texts and products. Although children's ability to creatively use structured toys does not exonerate the toys' creators for imbuing them with problematic attributes, it does illustrate that for some children, these aspects are not the only significant ones. As adults, we are justified in acting as advocates and demanding healthier popular culture products for children. At the same time, however, we would be wise to be open-minded, to listen, and to bear witness to the many ways in which children circumvent and subvert the dominant attributes they encounter in children's culture. Remembering that children are not just victims, but active agents with resilience and the ability to empower themselves, is especially crucial to our work as scholars.

☙ ───────────────────────────────────

Rebecca Hains is a Professor of Media and Communication at Salem State University. She is the author of *Growing Up With Girl Power: Girlhood on Screen and in Everyday Life* (2012) and *The Princess Problem: Guiding Our Girls Through the Princess-Obsessed Years* (2014). She is also the co-editor of the volumes *Princess Cultures: Mediating Girls' Identities and Imaginations* (2015, with Miriam Forman-Brunell), *Cultural Studies of LEGO: More Than Just Bricks* (2019, with Sharon Mazzarella), and *The Marketing of Children's Toys: Critical Perspectives on Children's Consumer Culture* (2021, with Nancy Jennings).

───────────────────────────────────── ❧

Notes

1. All details have been taken from manufacturers' details on Amazon.com.
2. All names have been changed.

References

American Psychological Association. 2007. *Report of the APA Task Force on the Sexualization of Girls.* <http://www.apa.org/pi/women/programs/girls/report.aspx> (accessed 28 September 2011).

duCille, Ann. 1994. "Dyes and Dolls: Multicultural Barbie and the Merchandizing of Difference." *Differences: A Journal of Feminist Cultural Studies* 6, no. 1: 47–68.

duCille, Ann. 1996. *Skin Trade.* Cambridge, MA: Harvard University Press.

Durham, Meenakshi Gigi. 2008. *The Lolita Effect: The Media Sexualization of Young Girls and What We Can Do About It.* Woodstock, NY: Overlook Press.

Hains, Rebecca C. 2012. *Growing Up With Girl Power: Girlhood On Screen and in Everyday Life.* New York: Peter Lang.

Guerrero, Lisa. 2009. "Can the Subaltern Shop? The Commodification of Difference in the *Bratz* Dolls." *Cultural Studies <=> Critical Methodologies* 9, no. 2: 186–196.

Kavilanz, Parija. 23 June 2011. "Bratz Are Back! Barbie Better Watch Out." *CNN Money.* <http://money.cnn.com/2011/06/22/news/companies/bratz_barbie_dolls_war/index.htm> (accessed 28 September 20s11).

Kearney, Mary-Celeste. 2011. *Mediated Girlhoods: New Explorations of Girls' Media Culture.* New York: Peter Lang.

LaFerla, Ruth. 26 October 2003. "Underdressed and Hot: Dolls Moms Don't Love." *The New York Times.* <http://www.nytimes.com/2003/10/26/style/noticed-under dressed-and-hot-dolls-moms-don-t-love.html?ref=bratzdoll> (accessed 28 September 2011).

Lamb, Sharon, and Lyn Mikel Brown. 2006. *Packaging Girlhood: Rescuing our Daughters from Marketers' Schemes.* New York: St. Martin's.

McAllister, Matthew P. 2007. "'Girls with a Passion for Fashion': The Bratz Brand as Integrated Spectacular Consumption." *Journal of Children and Media* 1, no. 3: 244–258.

Meltz, Barbara F. 11 Dec. 2003. "Super Sexy Fashion Dolls are Asking for Trouble." *The Boston Globe.* <http://www.boston.com/yourlife/family/articles/2003/12/11/super_sexy_fashion_dolls_are_asking_for_trouble/> (accessed 8 October 2011).

Orr, Lisa. 2009. "'Difference That Is Actually Sameness Mass-Reproduced': Barbie Joins the Princess Convergence." *Jeunesse: Young People, Texts, Cultures* 1, no 1: 9–30.

Riley, Charles. 21 April 2011. "Mattel Loses Bratz Case." <http://money.cnn.com/2011/04/21/news/companies/mattel_bratz_mga/index.htm?iid=EL> (accessed 28 September 2011).

Talbott, Margaret. 4 Dec. 2006. "Department of Marketing: Little Hotties." *The New Yorker.* <http://www.newyorker.com/archive/2006/12/04/061204fa_fact_talbot> (accessed 28 September 2011).

Valdivia, Angharad N. 2011. "This Tween Bridge Over my Latina Girl Back: The U.S. Mainstream Negotiates Ethnicity." Pp. 93–112 in *Mediated Girlhoods: New Explorations of Girls' Media Culture,* ed. M.-C. Kearney. New York: Peter Lang.

Wertheimer, Sophie. 2006. "Pretty in Panties: Moving Beyond the Innocent Child Paradigm in Reading Preteen Modeling Websites." Pp. 208–226 in *Girlhood: Redefining the Limits,* ed. Y. Jiwani, C. Steenburgen, and C. Mitchell. Montreal, Canada: Black Rose Press.

Chapter 7

Some Assembly Required
Black Barbie and the Fabrication of Nicki Minaj

Jennifer Dawn Whitney

CRO

Introduction

Wide-eyed and voluptuous, hip hop sensation Nicki Minaj poses on
the cover of her 2010 debut studio album, *Pink Friday*.[1] Donned in
a super-sleek pink wig, hot pink lipstick, shiny pink lace-up platform
boots, and a shimmering corseted dress winged in tulle, the songstress
sits propped, pouting for the camera. Showcased by a bubblegum-pink
backdrop, Minaj is surrounded by an overabundance of visual cues sig-
naling a girlishly sexy femininity. To accentuate this indulgent spec-
tacle, the photograph has been digitally modified. Minaj's legs are
elongated into caricature, her arms erased in their entirety. What results
is an archetypal picture of feminine excess. The new princess of hip hop

gazes out at her fans as a hyperfeminine and hyper-real representation of a dismembered black Barbie doll.[2]

With promotion from her record label, Young Money Entertainment, Minaj amplifies this doll-like image with a name and pastiched persona, extending it beyond photoshoots and album covers. "Harajuku Barbie," Minaj (2009a) explains, combines her appreciation of Tokyo street culture and its "free-spirited, girls just wanna have fun, kick ass"[3] attitude with the iconic status of the Barbie doll. Such influences manifest in the artist's public performance of her celebrity, which she accessorizes with stylized, multi-colored wigs, pink lipstick, a cute wardrobe, and affected voices. In many publicity photos, Minaj flashes a sparkly necklace with the word "Barbie" scrawled in its familiar cursive script. She explains the motivation behind co-opting the appearance of this cultural phenomenon, stating that, "all girls are Barbies. We all want to play dress-up" as well as be "icons and moguls"[4] (2009a).

This article will provide an analysis of Minaj's public persona with special reference to her playful appropriations. What follows is an investigation into the ways in which Minaj enacts a specific kind of Barbie doll-like hyperfemininity within the world of hip hop and popular, celebrity cultures. By examining the Barbie doll's racial, economic and historical underpinnings alongside Minaj's performance of these, this article also seeks to determine whether such appropriations erase the troublingly hegemonic narratives that surround the plastic doll, or whether such a performance leaves room for liberatory, pluralistic and feminist interpretations.

Where my Bitches at? Contextualizing the Fame of Nicki Minaj

Nicki Minaj's presence in hip hop, as Harajuku Barbie or otherwise, is exceptional. Women emcees have been involved in the scene since its inception, but the same level of commercial success as their male counterparts continues to be elusive. *Bitch Media* blogger, Alyx Vesey, highlights the dearth of women in the industry. She contends that Minaj's contemporaries, "like Lil Mama, Estelle, Ke$ha, and Kid Sister get some recognition, but not on the level that kingpins Jay-Z, Kanye West, T.I., and Lil Wayne receive" (2010: para. 9). She goes on to posit that women who were once hip hop superstars no longer sell records: "Older female rappers have either become less culturally relevant, like Missy Elliott, or have branched into a variety of creative and merchandising opportunities outside of hip hop, as Queen Latifah has done." When women artists do acquire mainstream recognition, as Latoya Peterson (2010) details for the website *Jezebel*, their "shelf life [in the] limelight is less than two years" (para.1). In such an intolerable climate, it is no wonder that when *Pink Friday* went platinum in 2011, it had been preceded by an eight-year drought for women in the business. (Lil' Kim previously achieved this accolade in 2003, with her album *La Bella Mafia*.) Minaj's acclaim has been met with a backlash that questions her talent and authenticity.[5] However, the rapper's response to her mainstream triumphs is in keeping with the exuberance of her Harajuku Barbie persona. At the news that sales of *Pink Friday* had surpassed Kanye West's *My Dark Beautiful Twisted Fantasy*, she exclaimed, "Girl Power! I deserve it this time" (Goddessjaz 2011: para. 3).

In *The Hip Hop Wars* (2008) cultural critic and African American studies scholar, Tricia Rose, discusses the complex issues women emcees face in hip hop. She asserts that in the industry, "sexism is visible, vulgar, aggressive and popular" (114). As a result, women artists are disenfranchised, and successful female rappers often follow a specific script. Rose (2008) elaborates on this, insisting that, "[T]hose who survived the commercial demands have relied on the product reserved especially for black women: sexual excess" (124). While Minaj's Barbie role-playing suggests the sexual excess that Rose describes, in the last decade there have been few other avenues for women in hip hop that also ensure similar levels of stardom. Accordingly, Minaj has expressed frustration and ambivalence at the way her persona is sometimes received by the public. In a profile piece for *Out* magazine, Caryn Ganz (2010) writes that Minaj decided "to fend off pervy guys stalking her online by playing to her female fans." Instead of catering to a male audience, Minaj explains, "I started making it my business to say things that would empower women, like, 'Where my bitches at?' to let them know, 'I'm here for you,'" she says (1).

Crucially, Minaj seems to be occupying several recognizable roles in the tradition of women's hip hop. Ethnomusicology scholar Cheryl Keyes (2004) explains that "four distinct categories of women rappers emerge in rap music performance." She defines these as "Queen

Mother," "Fly Girl," "Sista with Attitude," and "Lesbian" (306). While Minaj might be remiss in playing out the "Queen Mother" role, wherein rappers "view themselves as African-centered icons," she does mediate among the other three. "Fly Girls" are rappers who dress "in chic clothing and fashionable hairstyles, jewelry and cosmetics" (309), though many inhabit more than one archetypal role at a time. Keyes describes the significance of the "Fly Girl" as "far more than a whim, for it highlights aspects of black women's bodies considered undesirable by American mainstream standards of beauty" (310). Such performances can be understood as "'flippin da script' (deconstructing dominant ideology) by wearing clothes that accent" parts of the anatomy "considered beauty markers of Black women by Black culture" (310). Minaj's mode of adornment which recalls Barbie's "chic clothing and fashionable hairstyles, jewelry and cosmetics" (309) if not Barbie's hegemonically defined anatomy, presents her fans with an interesting ambivalence in which the "Fly Girl" is balanced against the model doll.

Identifying Minaj's performance with that of a "Fly Girl" indicates only a fraction of her constructed persona. Keyes demarcates "Sista with Attitude" as the next category, wherein women emcees "value attitude as a means of empowerment." To enhance this attitude, many "Sistas," she explains, "have reclaimed the word *bitch*" (original emphasis) in order to "subvert patriarchal rule" (312). Minaj has embraced the extremes in both attitude and vocabulary of the "Sista" without much hesitation. However, significantly, she follows on from a shift that Keyes suggests moved away from the overtly political. In the mid- to late 1990s, Keyes explains that the "Sista" category "was augmented with rappers Lil' Kim and Foxy Brown who conflate fly and hardcore attitudes in erotic lyrics and video performances" (313). These new arrivals were often associated with male-dominated crews, and were frequently accused of "misusing sex and feminism and devaluing Black men" (313), all of which have been criticisms of Minaj as well.

Minaj demonstrates a body confidence and creative aesthetic that connects her to the "Fly Girl." Her lyrics, asserting that she has "the fattest pussy in the business" (2008) indicate a provocative swagger in line with the "Sista with Attitude." However, Minaj holds the most complex relationship with Keyes' final type of woman in hip hop, the "Lesbian." For Keyes, this figure is out both lyrically and publicly: Minaj seems to shift in and out of this position in mercurial fashion. The rapper has not publicly identified as a lesbian, but her sexual identity is not that straightforward either. In "Go Hard" she raps, "I only stop for pedestrians or a real, real bad lesbian" (2009b). Many other lyrics, full of similar posturing, suggest that her (fictional?) sexual conquests are often women.[6]

What is striking about the three out of four archetypes of women in hip hop in which Minaj navigates, is that they all stress the importance of sexuality. While such categories do suggest empowerment, Rose (2008) discusses the challenges in offering a feminist reading:

> Not all black women's sexually explicit material is feminist, anti-patri-archal or empowering. In fact, the women who have been elevated as mainstream commercial rappers over the past ten years generally follow the larger pattern of hypersexualized, objectified terms reserved for black women in the genre. Highly visible rappers like Lil' Kim, Trina, and Foxy Brown use the black female-required sex card in hip hop; their stories of so-called sexual power generate from using their sexuality as the basis for their image. (123–124)

Rose (2008) goes on to caution that while an emphasis on the sexually explicit can be liberatory, it also risks aligning with the "mainstream" and racist idea "that black women [are] sexually excessive and deviant as a class of women" (115). Considering this context, the manufacture of the Harajuku Barbie persona, the Nicki Minaj celebrity performance, and the conflation of the two, can be viewed as residing within an oft-enacted script. While Minaj's proclamation of "Girl Power," her uninhibited pleasure in costume play and performance, and her bicurious lyrics are affiliated with feminist, postmodern and queer politics, are these simply materialist antics accentuating a hypersexuality which, in turn, is meant to fix the attention of a wider audience? Is Minaj's performance a fabrication of edgy and brash sex appeal designed to seduce fans into buying more records?

The *Out* article dedicated to Minaj speculates on her popular appeal. Comparing Minaj to Lady Gaga, Ganz (2010) muses that the latter's "audience was primed to accept her as a sexually adventurous nonconformist by artists like Madonna and David Bowie." In contrast, she contends that, "in hip-hop, Nicki Minaj is a real space oddity." She expands on this: "Rap has never seen a mainstream rising star this eccentric and brave, yet for all of Minaj's curious artistic choices (two-tone wigs, spontaneous British dialects, shout-outs to *Harry Potter*) she's also incredibly popular" (2010). Minaj is often compared to Lady Gaga. They are both outrageous, larger-than-life figures who alter traditional conceptions of femininity and sexuality until they are almost unrecognizable. Their fans adore them for it, and their critics attempt to pass them off as copycats, insisting that Gaga simply reproduces the creative stylings of Madonna and David Bowie, while Minaj is a replica of the aforementioned Lil' Kim.[7]

Given her predilection for material excess, it is somewhat of a surprise that Lady Gaga and Nicki Minaj diverge when it comes to Barbie. Whenever a Barbie doll was tossed onstage during Gaga's The Monster Ball Tour, the performer took to decapitating it. Upon removing its head—often with her teeth—Gaga would then express her disdain for the plaything, informing her devoted fans, much to their delight, that Barbie perpetuates an impossible feminine ideal. While such an act and accompanying message exercises a type of feminist defiance, perhaps Gaga's stunt also can be read as a colonizing move by a white feminist. Gaga must be aware of Minaj's Barbie doll-influence on her fans. These fans, or "Barbies/Barbz," as they collectively refer to themselves, are often girls and women of color who identify with the brand of femininity Gaga disparages. As such, this mischievous display also might be contextualized as an act of violence. In attempting to dismantle particular narratives of gender conformity, then, Gaga simultaneously alienates Minaj's fans—and their crossover audience—through the beheading of the plastic doll.

It is without doubt that Minaj's fans have received Harajuku Barbie with enthusiasm, and it does not appear that Lady Gaga will sway them. With Minaj's support, keen followers have been happily brandishing the Barbie moniker, inspired by the star to interpret this style and attitude in new and inventive ways. As such, a fan-organized Barbie Movement has taken shape. With it, online communities document both Minaj's doll-like persona as well as that of her fans. Fan-created blogs display discussions about beauty and fashion, and provide helpful tips to achieve the Barbie aesthetic, while an endless stream of inspirational images of Minaj circulate.[3] MyPinkFriday.com, the rapper's official website, also hosts forums where fans can communicate. In a thread offering support and friendship to self-identified Barbz, one fan expresses her enthusiasm in being a "diva" (2011). Conversely, another fan (2011) bemoans being called "fake." As well as being an intimate online community, the Barbz certainly have commercial sway. In December 2010, they began to motivate for Minaj and Mattel—the corporation behind Barbie—to collaborate in order to create an official Nicki Minaj Barbie doll. In December 2011, their wish was granted with a doll modeled after Minaj's *Pink Friday* album cover.

Popular critics have been quick to denounce the spirited enthusiasm of both Minaj and her fans as misdirected attempts at feminism-lite, or worse, expressing valid concern in a similar vein to Rose's assessment. Convincing arguments have been established that the rapper and her ilk are perpetuating Orientalism, and/or contributing to the oversexualization of women in hip hop (see Jenn 2010; Vesey 2010). When Minaj performed alongside Mariah Carey in a remixed edition of the song "Up Out My Face," both appearing as Barbie dolls in the video, such analysis was acute (Vesey 2010). However, Minaj easily articulates an explanation of her representation, and how her fans choose to assimilate this expression. She declares that she is a role model for young girls (Weiner 2010), and as Gantz (2010) details,

> Minaj definitely has a lot to say about the politics of being a woman in the 21st-century music biz. "Everybody knows I can go out and pick a dude and date him," she says. "But I want to do what people think I can't do, which is have the number 1 album in the country and be the first female rapper to sell records like dudes in this day and age." After taking some heat for identifying with one of the best-selling, and most disproportioned, toys in history—she ends phone calls with a screeched "It's Barbie, *bitch!*"—she was accused of being plastic. "It's interesting that people have more negative things to say about me saying 'I'm Barbie' than me saying 'I'm a bad bitch,'" she says, getting a bit heated. "So you can call yourself a female dog because that's cool in our community. But if you call yourself a Barbie, that's fake." (2)

Minaj clearly understands her hyperfeminine performance of Harajuku Barbie to be playful as well as empowering. Further, as Vesey contends, "there may be something celebratory about Minaj's appropriation of an eminent symbol of white femininity" (Vesey 2010: para. 3).

It's Barbie, Bitch! Re-defining the Doll

Nicki Minaj's relationship with, and co-option of, the Barbie brand of femininity complicates the traditional feminist perspective of the doll and her far-reaching influence. Natasha Walter, a feminist journalist and nonfiction writer, highlights this perspective in her latest book. *Living Dolls* (2010) offers a popular analysis of the contemporary culture of girls and young women in the West. In it, she worries: "It often seems that now the dolls are escaping from the toy shop and taking over girls' lives" (2). Walter's concern is that many girls and young women have a desire to be doll-like, and this can have a dangerous effect on their self-esteem and body image. Rather than adhering to this conceptualization of what it means to be doll-like, however, Minaj toys with it. In the process, instead of simply internalizing the hegemony Walter discusses, Minaj and the Barbie Movement hold potential to interrogate, subvert and redefine the traditional tropes of Barbie doll-like white femininity.

Vesey (2010) ponders whether "the aspiration [to imitate Barbie by way of Minaj] results from some black girls wanting to find dolls with whom they can identify" (para. 4). This question offers insight into the scarcity of convincingly diverse Barbie doll options. Significantly, analyses of Barbie and race often suggest that while Barbie dolls do come in many different colors, there remains one, iconic Barbie. As Mary Rogers, author of the critical reader *Barbie Culture* (1999), posits through a reading of feminist and queer theorist Erica Rand, media and visual texts that contain representations of Barbie "convey the message *not* that any girl can be like Barbie, but that *any* girl can be like Barbie's friend" (56 emphases in original). Regardless of whether Mattel has created black dolls that bear the name Barbie, in these advertisements and visual narratives, the real and true Barbie is always white—with an assortment of diverse friends. Thus, when Rogers later writes that, "Barbie is an icon whose 'perfect' body is more attainable than ever before," (122) what is implied here is that her body is more attainable for young, affluent, white women. Considering this, what then happens if girls and women of color decide that they, too, will appropriate attributes of the Barbie doll?

In the case of Minaj and Harajuku Barbie, there is an inevitable cultural backlash. One example, worth exploring further here, involves recent white pop/rap phenomenon and internet it-girl, Kreayshawn (2011). In her self-produced track, "Gucci, Gucci" she spits the lyrics "Bitch, you ain't no Barbie," purportedly accusing Minaj and her fans of failing to achieve doll-like perfection. When asked to address this for Complex.com, Kreayshawn justifies her lyrics thus:

> Honestly man, this is no disrespect to [Minaj] because she's got talent. She's got an image. But when it comes to inspiring young women, her message is to be a Barbie—to be plastic, to be fake, to all have blonde hair (Ahmed 2011: para.3).

Kreayshawn condemns Minaj for a lack of authenticity, but she, too, could be accused of adopting an inauthentic persona. A member of the controversially named White Girl Mob, Kreayshawn, born Natassia Gail Zolot, seems to be appropriating an ethnicized stage name in order to connect with a hip hop audience. Perhaps such accusations are not simply acrimonious, but reside within a larger context.

Feuding in hip hop has a long and notorious history. Popular culture blogger, Goddessjaz, explains that, "Public 'beef' is a hugely powerful promotional tool and can make or break careers" (2011). Indeed, while Kreayshawn may have provoked a rivalry with Minaj, the latter was already embroiled in another feud with Lil' Kim. Critics have much to say about this tradition, especially when a feud occurs between women. Goddessjaz (2011) pointedly queries: "But what does it mean when the few women on the mainstream scene are bickering?" (para. 5). Likewise, when race enters into the debate, it creates further questions. Would Kreayshawn have thought it necessary to criticize Minaj's Barbie doll-like qualities—or, crucially, what she understands as a lack thereof—if Minaj were not a woman of color? Kreayshawn's comments exist within a tradition of feuding in hip hop, but they should not be read merely as part of the business. Such remarks are situated within a wider cultural narrative that repeatedly insists that black girls and women cannot be Barbie doll-like. Further, this discourse troublingly implies that, like the black Barbie dolls to which they are equated, Minaj and her fans are simply counterfeit imitations of a blonde original.

The ubiquity of the original, white Barbie doll, and the assumed inauthenticity of the black Barbie doll, deserves a closer look. In her book *Girls* (2002) Catherine Driscoll asserts that, despite her clear and recognizable signification, "Barbie is never complete" (98). While the doll is laden with the meaning imparted by five decades of creators and consumers alike, in her there is a certain blankness that enables inter-pretive versatility. It is from this ambiguous space that Barbie assumes the flexibility to occupy fantasies, uphold innumerable and conflict-ing representations of identity, and redefine the meaning she suppos-edly embodies. Rand, in *Barbie's Queer Accessories* (1995) reasons that,

"Mattel touts Barbie as a catalyst for fantasy and since the 1960s has deliberately refrained from circulating certain Barbie biographical details or narratives—such as age, a geographical location, or a wedding—that might foreclose fantasy options" (8). Thus, while Barbie's signification may never be complete, she is not simply an empty signifier upon which meaning can be written. It is through Mattel's meticulous engineering and advertising ingenuity that Barbie's narrative persists as enigma. As such, this incompleteness is incorporated into her branded narrative.

Since Mattel holds specific information about Barbie strategically under wraps, this act of cloistering becomes inseparable from the very story that is cultivated to keep her contemporary—the primary objective of Mattel. Her body, hair, makeup, and fashion ensembles not only reflect the year in which she was manufactured, but they also work to maintain a superficial narrative that Rand (1995) describes: in 1959 "Barbie [began] as a good girl." Now she represents "a paragon of feminism and diversity in their most widely palatable, and co-opted, forms" (193). It is through a combination of attention to detail and subtlety that Barbie remains relevant to shifting ideas of femininity, yet is always narratively secure. The incompleteness that Driscoll describes is a calculated feature which functions both to belie and reinforce the elasticity of Barbie's image. It is a well-crafted singular representation to which Barbie always returns, while appearing slightly rejuvenated each year that she re-emerges.

Ann duCille (1994) elaborates on this marketing strategy in her essay "Dyes and Dolls." She argues that Mattel's ventures maintain Barbie's original white, able-bodied status, which is never in question despite the blankness (read whiteness) attributed to her. Indeed, duCille states that Mattel's proliferation of diverse representations of Barbie, including a plethora of racial and ethnic identities, work to perpetuate these "different" dolls precisely as other. Addressing dolls specifically racialized by Mattel as black, she argues that these Barbies are simply "dye-dipped versions of archetypal white American beauty" (49). She explains that, "Regardless of what color the dolls are dipped in or what costumes they are adorned with, the image they present is of the same mythically thin, long-legged, luxuriously haired, buxom beauty" (50). Speaking to the historical process of both manufacturing and naming these dolls, Rand elucidates this point. She recalls that, "In the 1960s, there were 'nonethnic' Barbie and her sometimes 'ethnic' friends" (1995: 83). While today, "some 'ethnic' dolls now get the name *Barbie*, a 'nonethnic' Barbie still occupies center stage, and only she can do anything" (83–84). Rand specifies that if "there can only be one" Barbie "she's white and blonde." The variety of skin tones Mattel has created "are merely temporary costumes that Barbie puts on in certain situations, and importantly, that you can buy" (84). Thus, both duCille and Rand (1995) contend that while Mattel has been creating and producing an array of visually different Barbie dolls, such production works to reinforce the discourse that there is only one real Barbie doll, and she is white.

Today, not all ethnic Barbies are dye-dipped versions of the original. Since the 1990s Mattel has been making head and face moulds representative of the ethnicity each doll is designed to embody. Yet the company's attempts to be progressively more diverse remain problematic at best. More recent designs by Mattel, such as the So-In-Style Barbie dolls released in the summer of 2009, again make an effort to encompass black identity: "Courtney, the cheerleader doll, has a fuller nose and fuller lips than regular Barbie. Trichelle, the doll 'into art and journalism,' has curly hair; Kara who loves math and music, has a 'darker' skin tone"[9] (Stewart 2009: para. 2). Even with these latest versions of Barbie's black friends, however, the white, blonde and busty Barbie continues to be enforced as the authentic, true and original doll, exemplifying the all-American norm to which all other dolls must measure up.

With the celebration of Barbie's fiftieth year in 2009, festivities in the world of celebrity—from runway shows to magazine editorials—commemorated the original white doll's impact on popular culture. Richard Dyer, in his book *White* (1997) describes how such occurrences work at normalizing whiteness and perpetuating racial hegemony. He explains that

> [a]s long as race is something only applied to non-white peoples, as long as white people are not racially seen and named, they/we function as a human norm. Other people are raced, we are just people. ... This assumption, that white people are just people, which is not far off saying that whites are people whereas other colours are something else, is endemic to white culture (1–2).

Thus, when, in a fictive interview with *Forbes*, the original white Barbie proclaims, "I am a big believer in dreaming big and inspiring girls that they can do anything they set their minds to" (Vander Broek 2009:

para. 2), it seems like a contradiction; Barbie's ethnic doll counterparts are always a high-heeled step behind. As Mattel persists with Barbie's twenty-first century image as progressive, feminist and multicultural, so long as there is one Barbie to which all other Barbies must refer, such attempts will continue to gloss over issues of whiteness as a non-race, and, in turn, sustain white as the norm to which Dyer attests.

In terms of manufacturing and marketing, Barbie resides in an awkward position: Mattel withholds biographical information to encourage fantasy, while simultaneously producing an overflow of diverse fantasy representations. Such representations are dubious, for they may not be understood as representations of identity at all. Rather, race and ethnicity, while reflecting particularities of identities, are being marketed as accessories to the original. Further, as Mattel continues to manufacture ethnic-looking dolls alongside the original, white Barbie, additional questions emerge about racial authenticity. Critically, as duCille (1994) reflects:

> The notion that fuller lips, broader noses, wider hips, and higher derrières somehow make the Shani dolls more realistically African American raises many difficult questions about authenticity, truth, and the ever-problematic categories of the real and the symbolic, the typical and the stereotypical. Just what are we saying when we claim that a doll does or does not 'look black?' (56)

In "Eating the Other," bell hooks (1992) takes up these issues of the commerce of diversity and authenticity. She argues that while contemporary marketing may be promoted with a "postmodern slant" (22) that appears to celebrate diversity and difference, such "commodification of Otherness" (21) reveals a nostalgia for racial authenticity. She insists that where representations of ethnic identities are introduced into the marketplace, there is a "resurgence of essentialist cultural nationalism [wherein, the] acknowledged Other must assume recognizable forms" (26). According to hooks, these forms often take shape in the primitive. As such, dolls such as the Shani Barbie that duCille describes exemplify what Mattel envisions black dolls to be—complete with African print clothing—and limit black bodies in mass culture to the atavistic.

Both duCille and hooks trouble the idea that identity is fixed, insisting that representations of race and ethnicity can no longer reside in something essentially authentic. While Minaj's Barbie doll-like performance begins to align with this analysis, attempts by Mattel to present an authentic racial accuracy do not take account of shifting definitions of identities in culture. Instead, they work to uphold a culturally specific, single moment in such identities. Mattel's approach prevents the possibility of fluidity of difference, and as hooks argues, "difference is often fabricated in the interests of social control as well as of commodity innovation" (25). She continues:

> The commodification of difference promotes paradigms of consumption wherein whatever difference the Other inhabits is eradicated *via* exchange by a consumer cannibalism that not only displaces the Other but denies the significance of that Other's history through a process of decontextualization (31).

As this applies to Barbie, Mattel has situated itself within a dilemma in which, in its efforts to make the doll more diverse, accessible, and therefore more marketable, it has also become more locked into stereotypes and static representations. These, in turn, work to negatively heighten and reinforce difference in one sense, while decontextualizing it in another. Thus, Mattel's efforts to transform the doll into an ethnic body may be doing multiple disservices to the children for whom it is a play and fantasy object. Certainly, duCille's sentiment that "Barbie's body type constructs the bodies of other women as deviant" (1994: 64) is not unorthodox, but this, alongside questions of race and ethnicity further raises the questions: Can Mattel ever physically represent ethnic and racial identity in its dolls? And, if not, what does it mean that white Barbie is successful at embodying a certain blank signifier that proliferates the notion of whiteness as invisible and thus the norm?

These questions persist within a Western context, and, increasingly, they also take precedence within an ever-growing global consumerist culture. As Barbie's popularity continues to move outside of the West, her subsequent influence has extended to global popular culture. Susie Orbach, on the subject of consumerism, succinctly argues in her popular book *Bodies* (2009) that, "Globalism brings uniformity to visual culture" (88). Here, she speaks to the anxiety that idealized white femininity may have a universalizing effect on global identities. However, the issue of Barbie's influence should not simply be understood as universalizing. As Driscoll (2002) attests,

> It may be useful to argue that Barbie imposes undesirable models of femininity on girls, but it is also the dominant public discourse on girls

> who like to play Barbie. It is not radical to imply that Barbie enthusi-
> asts are co-opted or stupid or to see Barbie as an ideological template,
> because these criticisms of girl culture are proper to positioning girls as
> definitively malleable gullible consumers. (98)

While it is worthwhile to critique the production and marketing of
Barbie, it would be a mistake to assume that consumers are limited
to interactions with Barbie dolls based simply on appearance, or the
incomplete fantasies Mattel manufactures. When Lady Gaga (2011)
preaches to her audience, and when Kreayshawn insists that Minaj
is perpetuating a message that "all" girls should "have blonde hair"
(Ahmed 2011: para. 3) like Barbie, they are reiterating the universalizing consequences of a singular Barbie doll fantasy.

Playtime's Not Over: The Possibilities of Harajuku Barbie

Critiques of Nicki Minaj imply that her Barbie doll-like persona is
most abhorrent in terms of being "plastic" and "fake" (Ahmed 2011:
para. 3). However, Minaj has decisively embraced these labels. Try as
she might, Kreayshawn, for example, is not disrespecting Minaj, but re-
articulating what the rapper has already made abundantly clear. Minaj
fully indulges in the material excess of the hyper-real Harajuku Barbie.
She plays up this larger than life persona lyrically, aurally, and visually.
Harajuku Barbie manifests in Minaj's songs, videos and photoshoots,
and Minaj seems to take pleasure in how technology is used to reshape
and redefine the lengths she is physically willing to go to.

Significantly, Harajuku Barbie, though Minaj's most prominent
persona, is not her only one. She shifts between several others including "Roman," "Rosa," and "Martha." Each of these personalities mate-
rializes in interviews, or while Minaj is rapping, and can be detected as
she changes accent and body language to accommodate the character.
What is also noteworthy here is that Minaj's biography is inconsistent,
at best. While her lyrics might suggest hypersexuality and bicuriosity,
Minaj insists in interviews that she does not date women, or men (Ganz
2010). There have also been discrepancies involving her age as well as
her upbringing. And, most befittingly, Minaj's legal surname is Maraj.
There is so much evidence to support Kreayshawn's claim that Minaj
is fake, that instead of its being an accusation, it is simply a statement

of the obvious. Considering this, like Vesey (2010), I too am "inclined to read this stylistic choice as an indication of the fragmented nature of female identities" (para. 11).

Rather than attempting to uncover a sort of true or real feminine identity, Minaj's multiple and fragmented self-interpretation, by way of Harajuku Barbie, offers keen insight into an alternative understanding. Minaj's brand of Barbie doll-like femininity both imitates and parodies the iconic doll, going beyond straightforward identification. Her gendered personas, pastiched performances, and hyperbolic revelry can be situated within a framework of poststructural and postmodern feminism, touched upon in the quotations by duCille (1992) and hooks (1994) above. In this tradition, the idea of an authentic and cohesive feminine identity is called into question. This logic is echoed throughout French feminisms of the twentieth century, where, most vocally, Simone de Beauvoir (1997) asserts that, "One is not born, but rather, becomes a woman" (295). Such ideas about the fluid nature of femininity have resonated with contemporary feminist philosophers, including Judith Butler. Butler (1999), in her influential research, insists that all gendered bodies are referential, or an "imitation without an origin" (175). These analyses, while building upon each other, have extended feminist debate by suggesting that there is no essential femininity. It is through this lens that a critical analysis of what is fake and what is real in terms of a Barbie doll-like femininity can take shape.

In her book, *Yes Means Yes,* Kath Albury (2002) is clearly influenced by Butler, as she develops her own ideas about femininity in new and exciting directions. In her analysis of what she calls "female female-impersonators," she observes the cliché that "[t]he ideal Western woman is pretty, witty, charming, sexy and blonde" (86). While this is not surprising, she asserts that "female female-impersonators" seek to "play out the 'dark' or 'ugly' side of the ideal" by taking it to a place of excess (86). When these women "assume angry, parodic roles, … they rub their audiences' noses in the messy fake that lies beneath the accepted myth of 'natural' femininity" (86). With this in mind, I see Minaj's performance of femininity as both apt and important. Her fragmented personas, and Barbie doll-like performances of excess reflect a gendered and sexualized configuration that reveals her femininity to be a parodic imitation. Through her performances, connections between natural and ideal femininity are revealed to be playful constructions. Minaj's multiple personas encompass a wide range of qualities and postures, from the conventionally pretty to the grotesque. As Edith Zimmerman (2010) writes for the feminist blog, *The Hairpin,* "somewhere along the line she clearly stopped caring whether or not she sounds 'pretty'" (para. 5) and instead delights in the vocally strange. In doing so, Minaj explicitly exposes the Barbie doll-like white femininity that she is parodying to be unnatural as well. Taking the idea of hyperfeminine parody into consideration as a site that is especially productive, Kim Toffoletti, in her critical work, *Cyborgs and Barbie Dolls* (2007) contends that Barbie, and the feminine bodies that inform and are informed by her, offers a textured interpretation of feminine subjectivity. It is her contention that Barbie is "an in-between phenomenon constantly circulating in the ambivalent space between the image and its referent, between illusion and the real." As such, both plastic and flesh-and-blood Barbies/Barbz call "established categories into question" (58). In this way, there is a transgressive engagement with feminine subjectivity, which Toffoletti asserts enables the subject to be perceived as transformative. She contends that, "Figurations such as Barbie, function to encourage alternative understandings of the body and self as transformative, rather than bound to an established system of meaning." She goes on to assert that Barbie, and those who appropriate her, offer the "potential for identity to be mutable and unfixed" (59). Toffoletti sees potential in what Barbie's plastic body offers real women by calling the very notion of what counts as real into question.

Arguments against Minaj's Barbie doll-like femininity, especially those that interrogate her authenticity, reinforce an essentialist paradigm. The undercurrent is that femininity is static, and ought to follow specific, well-prescribed rules. Such articulations insist that there is a natural, or truer state of femininity. Minaj liberates this convention with her persona of Harajuku Barbie, offering a thoroughly postmodern reading of, specifically, white femininity. Minaj's performance takes pleasure in the fragmentation and hyperbole of postmodern culture, as is envisioned through her stretched and broken limbs on the cover of *Pink Friday.* Through parody, she is undertaking the serious task of offering a critical conceptualization of the excesses that are inherent in consumer-based hip hop and celebrity culture, and, simultaneously putting forth a playful alternative to the static black Barbie doll representations imagined by Mattel. While the traditional

Barbie doll assumes a model of aspiration to a specific Western demographic, Minaj mischievously subverts the standard. The Barbie doll is refracted by Minaj's performance into an ever-changing plethora of behaviors and possibilities. In this sense, what is fake and plastic about Minaj, and what is fake and plastic about Barbie, become their greatest attributes.

CB

Jennifer Dawn Whitney is a lecturer at the University of South Wales where she teaches critical, contextual, and historical studies in fashion. Alongside her teaching, she researches and writes about representations of femininity in popular, material, and visual cultures—and is especially interested in the ways in which fashion, beauty, health, and technology intersect. Jennifer is the co-editor of *Dolls Studies: The Many Meanings of Girls' Toys and Play*. She is currently completing her first monograph, *Plastic Beauty: Dolls and the Construction of Modern Femininity*, to be published by Bloomsbury in 2021.

ED

Notes

1. The album cover art is available on Minaj's official website: <www.mypink friday.com> (accessed 10 January 2012).

2. Minaj is Trinidad-born and of mixed-race ancestry. She has self-identified as black in interviews and song lyrics. In popular media, she is repeatedly labeled "Black Barbie."

3. 0.53 seconds into the video: "Nicki Minaj Explains 'Harajuku Barbie'" Minaj's engagement with the Barbie side of her Harajuku Barbie persona is most often highlighted in visual and textual sources. As such, it is the focus here. Unfortunately beyond the scope of this article, an in depth investigation into Minaj's identification with, and assimilation of Harajuku street culture deserves further attention.

4. 1.10 minutes into the video: "Nicki Minaj Explains 'Harajuku Barbie'"

5. In depth analyses of issues of authenticity in hip hop can be found in "Part Two, 'No Time For Fake Niggas': Hip Hop Culture and the Authenticity Debates" in *That's the Joint!*

6. Troublingly, however, her verses are also peppered with the heterosexist shorthand "no homo" (Ganz 2010).

7. In 2000, Lil' Kim released the video for her single "How Many Licks?" wherein she played the role of a factory-assembled living doll. In July 2011, she posed as a real-life Barbie for a promotional photoshoot. Considering that Harajuku Barbie appears to have formed on the same assembly line as Kim's video persona, comparisons are frequent. As such, a rivalry between the rappers has developed.

8. Such fansites include: <http://bee-leed-dat-bitch.tumblr.com/>, <http://www
.facebook.com/nickiminaj>, <http://fuckyeahharajukubarbie.tumblr.com/>, <http://
hellyeahnickiminaj.tumblr.com/> and <http://nickiminajbarbies.com/> (accessed 10
January 2012).

9. An image of the So-In-Style dolls is available at: <http://www.barbie.com/
activities/friends/soinstyle/> (accessed 10 January 2012).

References

Ahmed, Insanul. 2011. "In Her Own Words: Who Is Kreayshawn?" <http://www
.complex.com/music/2011/05/who-is-kreayshawn/influences#gallery> (accessed
10 January 2012).

Albury, Kath. 2002. *Yes Means Yes: Getting Explicit About Heterosex*. Crows Nest, Aus-
tralia: Allen and Unwin.

Butler, Judith. 1999. *Gender Trouble*. New York and London: Routledge.

Carey, Mariah (featuring Nicki Minaj). 2010. "Up Out My Face." *Memoirs of an Im-
perfect Angel*. Island Records.

de Beauvoir, Simone. [1949] 1997. *The Second Sex*. Trans. H.M. Parshley. London:
Vintage.

Driscoll, Catherine. 2002. *Girls: Feminine Adolescence in Popular Culture and Cultural
Theory*. New York: Columbia University Press.

duCille, Ann. 1994. "Dyes and Dolls: Multicultural Barbie and the Merchandising of
Difference." *Differences* 6, no. 1: 46–68.

Dyer, Richard. 1997. *White: Essays on Race and Culture*. London and New York:
Routledge.

Ganz, Caryn. 2010. "The Curious Case of Nicki Minaj." <http://www.out.com/detail
.asp?page=2&id=27391> (accessed 10 January 2012).

Goddessjaz. 2011. "Nicki Minaj: 1st Female Platinum Rapper in 8 Years." <http://
feministing.com/2011/01/06/nicki-minaj-1st-female-platinum-rapper-in-8
-years/> (accessed 10 January 2012).

hooks, bell. 1992. "Eating the Other." Pp. 21–41 in *Black Looks: Race and Representation*. London: Turnaround.

Jenn (Guest Contributor). 2010. "The Orientalism of Nicki Minaj." <http://www
.racialicious.com/2010/11/01/the-orientalism-of-nicki-minaj/> (accessed   10
January 2012).

Keyes, Cheryl L. 2006. "Empowering Self, Making Choices, Creating Spaces: Black
Female Identity Via Rap Music Performance." Pp. 305–319 in *That's the Joint! The
Hip Hop Studies Reader*, eds. M. Forman and M.A. Neal. New York: Routledge.

Kreayshawn. 2011. "Gucci, Gucci." Sony Music Entertainment.

Lady Gaga. 2011. "Lady Gaga Decapitates Barbie." <http://www.youtube.com/watch
?v=acvIuOeKH5w> (accessed 10 January 2012).

Lil' Kim. 2000. "How Many Licks?" *The Notorious K.I.M.* Atlantic Records.

Minaj, Nicki. 2007. "Playtime is Over." *Playtime is Over*. Young Money Entertainment.

Minaj, Nicki (featuring Lil Wayne). 2008. "Lollipop [Remix]." *Sucka Free.* Young Money Entertainment.

Minaj, Nicki. 2009. "Nicki Minaj Explains 'Harajuku Barbie.'" <http://vimeo.com/6019791> (accessed 10 January 2012).

Minaj, Nicki. 2009. "Go Hard." *Beam Me Up Scotty.* Young Money Entertainment.

Mypinkfriday.com Fan Forum. "The Unfortunate Part About Being a Barbie." <http://mypinkfriday.com/forum/back/195261> (accessed 10 January 2012).

Orbach, Susie. 2009. *Bodies: Big Ideas.* London: Profile Books.

Peterson, Latoya. 2010. "Nicki Minaj and the Issue of Female MCs." <http://jezebel.com/5478800/nicki-minaj-and-the-issue-of-female-mcs> (accessed 10 January 2012).

Rand, Erica. 1995. *Barbie's Queer Accessories.* Durham: Duke University Press.

Rogers, Mary F. 1999. *Barbie Culture.* Thousand Oaks and London: Sage Publications.

Rose, Tricia. 2008. *The Hip Hop Wars: What We Talk About When We Talk About Hip Hop—And Why It Matters.* New York: Basic Books.

Stewart, Dodai. 2009. "Mattel's New Black Barbie a Step in the Right Direction." <http://jezebel.com/5315415/mattels-new-black-barbie-a-step-in-the-right-direction> (accessed 10 January 2012).

Toffoletti, Kim. 2007. *Cyborgs and Barbie Dolls: Feminism, Popular Culture and the Posthuman Body.* New York and London: I.B. Tuaris.

Vander Broek, Anna. 2009. "The Forbes Fictional Interview: Barbie." <http://www.forbes.com/2009/03/05/barbie-doll-interview-business_speaks.html?fd=rss_business> (accessed 10 January 2012).

Vesey, Alyx. 2010. "Tuning In: Nicki Minaj." <http://bitchmagazine.org/post/tuning-in-nicki-minaj> (accessed 10 January 2012).

Walter, Natasha. 2010. *Living Dolls: The Return of Sexism.* London: Virago Press.

Weiner, Jonah. 2010. "Who's That Girl?" <http://www.slate.com/articles/arts/music_box/2010/02/whos_that_girl.html> (accessed 10 January 2012).

Zimmerman, Edith. 2010. "Who is Nicki Minaj?" <http://thehairpin.com/2010/11/who-is-nicki-minaj> (accessed 10 January 2012).

Chapter 8

Black Girls and Dolls Navigating Race, Class, and Gender in Toronto

Janet Rosemarie Seow

❦

Introduction

Toys are important tools through which the social constructions of race, gender, and class are explored and enacted, particularly, but not exclusively, among children. Within a multicultural Canadian context, ethnic dolls have been criticized by a number of social and cultural theorists on the grounds that they promote racial stereotypes. Black dolls, in particular, have been criticized for their sexualization of black girls. Some ethnic dolls, including the Bratz doll line, have been criticized for their sexually suggestive attire that conveys a particular representation of black girls (see Bernstein (2011) and Doris Wilkinson (1974, 1987). My article focuses on black Barbie and other ethnic dolls in order to study the wider phenomenon of how black girls see the reality of their lives as compared to the lives of white girls.

I begin with a review of the historical and contemporary fields of black doll materiality that shows explicitly how the dominant group's perceptions of racialized characteristics are embedded in black doll culture, particularly in the Global North. I go on to describe the methodological approach I adopted in a participatory survey with a small group of girls and young women from Afro Caribbean communities in Toronto. Using their feedback, I then demonstrate how, in multicultural and multiracial Toronto, doll play is used by girls to effect resistance as well as to learn social rules, including norms and values related to race and gender performance.

Historical Background of Black Dolls in North America

The values of the dominant group have always influenced the collective imagination of what it means to conform. Black dolls are commonly viewed in contrast to the ideal white doll. I argue that this phenomenon is an offshoot of the colonial legacy with its roots in the early development of doll culture in North America. I draw on Robin Bernstein's (2011) research, in which she examines white children's play culture with black dolls to highlight the importance of race, class, and gender in the construction of the black child during the late eighteenth to mid-nineteenth centuries in America.

The most notable academic research on this topic was by psychologists Kenneth Clark and Mamie Clark (1947) who, in the 1940s, examined black children's relationships with white dolls. The children unanimously chose white dolls as their preferred friend. Clark and Clark concluded that black children were burdened with the effect of racial discrimination and a sense of inferiority. During the ensuing decades following this research, various representations of black dolls were created to mitigate earlier manifestations of racial inferiority in black doll culture. The aesthetic changes from dolls that had represented the black servant class to those that were now clearly representative of middle-class black people in the 1940s and 1950s were rejected by white families, the main consumers of black dolls at the time, as Sabrina Thomas (2007) points out. However, poor market sales did not stop the push to have positive representations in black doll culture. In 1980, the first African-American Barbie with Afro hair was released. Since then, a steady stream of ethnic dolls has been produced to appease an increasingly discerning market.

Maureen Trudelle Schwarz (2005) claims that the presence of ethnic dolls in the white doll market indicated the upward mobility of African-Americans at the time. She writes, "As the spending power of African-Americans and many other ethnic groups reached an all-time high in the 1980s and 1990s, toymakers' efforts at ethnic playthings were met with great enthusiasm and soaring profits" (296). Schwarz assumes that high marketing and consumption levels implied a shift in doll culture toward a popular way in which children could showcase their multiple identities, desires, and racial equality, but not everyone agrees that high consumption in the doll market correlates to an increase in black pride and social mobility. According to Ann duCille (1994), the marketing of difference through the consumption of ethnic dolls served the specific purpose of reinforcing the otherness of minorities. Visible differences such as skin tone and body shape become markers of otherness that bolstered what Mary Rogers (1999) described as white Barbie's iconic status as an unattainable ideal. This discourse remains relevant in contemporary black doll culture which is evident in the scarcity of black dolls and their subordinate position in terms of product availability and price.

Contemporary Ethnic Dolls

Ethnic dolls create a particular stigmatized understanding of minorities in the minds of the consuming public. In recent years, this stigma about the representations of ethnic dolls has been reinforced by criticisms in the media and in academic literature. For example, research is dominated by the study of the racially diverse Bratz dolls and the ethnic Barbie. In 2007, a study on the sexualization of dolls was commissioned by the American Psychological Association (APA). These researchers found evidence of sexualization in the representation and objectification of dolls. Bratz dolls were seen to be the most worrying; their race and highly sexualized clothing were being used, it was believed, to promote the negatively perceived otherness of visible minorities.

Other research (see Whitney 2012) has also driven home the similar point that intrinsic to the Bratz image is the promotion of an urban lifestyle and a hip-hop culture, both of which are strongly linked to deviance and, therefore, to black and Latino communities. Ann duCille (1994) sees African-American Barbie as a mere facsimile of the original white Barbie dipped in dye. For her, this was a marketing ploy to commodify blackness and reinforce otherness. Findings from these theorists show how the cultural politics surrounding diverse girlhoods is reinforced by underpinning discourses of exclusion based on race, class, and ethnicity. In this article, I introduce a broader perspective by recognizing the motivations and subjective values of girls and young women as social actors as they navigate the sexual stereotypes and perceptions of low educational aspirations and achievements linked to black girls.

Methodology

My methodology is informed by Elizabeth Chin's (1999) and Rebecca Hains's (2012) qualitative research projects that examine the effects of doll culture, race, representation, and consumption on the social world of inner-city black girls along with Hains's exploration of the function of role-playing and how dolls' racial diversity aids young girls' adaptability in negotiating issues such as racial identity, racism, and history. Also useful here is Chin's analysis of the correlation between socio-economic variables, consumption patterns, and girls' agency in circumventing their exclusion from the Western perception of girlhood. My study adopted a rights-based framework that relied on appropriate participatory research methods and methodologies that value the individual experiences of the participants (see Alderson and Morrow 2011; Chakraborty 2009; Ennew 2009). Ethical considerations related to working with girls are equally important (see Bushin 2007; James 2007).

As mentioned above, I worked with 10 girls and young women between the ages of 7 and 18 from Afro-Caribbean migrant communities in urban Toronto. These participants were from diverse socio-economic situations with some families comfortably middle-class and others self-identifying as belonging to lower socio-economic communities. The purpose of the project was explained to participants and their parents. Written informed consent forms were given to all parties, permission was obtained to use their images, and pseudonyms were adopted to protect confidentiality. I believed that interviewing the girls at home would increase their comfort level enough to allow them to open up about doll play and discuss their doll's special features such as hair and clothes. Capturing the essence of the girls' talk about race and doll play required a special self-reflexivity about a number of ethical issues, including my own position as an adult researcher and member of a visible minority. I was mindful that race talk might be embellished for me as the researcher. This perceived problem was alleviated through the use of multiple participatory methods. My methodology mostly used one-on-one activities and participant observation in order to maintain a trusting relationship with the girls. Equally important was my recognition that children are competent social actors and that they describe their life experiences in their own ways. This perspective of the girls' voices added to my understanding of their unique social world (see Alderson and Morrow 2011; James 2007). This meant that through doll-play, the girls were working significantly with me as informants and as researchers of their own lives. Their participation was directed in accordance with Articles 12 and 13 of the United Nations Convention on the Rights of the Child, (UNCRC)—the right to express their opinions and the more general right to freedom of expression.

Black Girls and Doll Play in Urban Toronto

All the participants owned several dolls, including Barbie dolls. Some had both black and white Barbies. A number of themes emerged from the interviews and small group discussions, including physical representation and the availability of ethnic dolls. For these participants, the most popular dolls were white Barbie, Bratz, My Scene, and American Girl. Like Chin's (1999), my respondents indicated that some ethnic dolls are not anatomically correct. They articulated an awareness of the white-normative cultural understanding of race that is displayed through the existence of limited and unimaginative racially different dolls. Black Barbie, not the most popular doll, was not perceived by Ashley and Sabrina, both 12 years of age, as a credible response to the need for equal representation.

Illustration 8.1 • Jennifer with her My Scene doll. Photo credit Janet Seow.

Janet: Do you think that a black Barbie is the same as a white Barbie?

Ashley: Yes, they're both the same. Nothing's really different. They just look different.

Janet: How different?

Ashley: One is just darker and one is just lighter.

Sabrina: Basically, I think it's just the skin color that's different because the physical features are like the same and the hair is the same … so they're just changing color, nothing's different.

Participants problematized the racially limited scope of Barbie culture in the same vein as did duCille (1994). Jennifer, for example, who was 18, contextualized black Barbie's arrival in the 1960s in terms of the race politics of the time.

Jennifer: That whole time period introduced the black Barbie … I don't like that, but I do like multicultural representation, but I don't like just black and white because the world isn't black and white, y'know there are so many different races, different colors. That's why I love the My Scene[1] dolls so much because there was the Hispanic girl … There are so many different kinds of people … I don't like the black and white thing.

Although the question presented to Jennifer presupposes a binary understanding of race, her analysis astutely expressed her frustration with the two-race argument and she chose to move beyond this. According to Jennifer, the emergence of black Barbie was a limited attempt at addressing multiculturalism in white terms, which reflects a limited racial complexity and a polarizing understanding of us and them. Jennifer's perception of past racial tapestries, such as the civil rights movements in the late 1960s, effectively summarizes some very current issues around race relations in North America and her own realities in multicultural Toronto. What Jennifer did not see is black Barbie as white. This might be because of her own biracial identity since she would never be seen as white either. When 7-year-old Stephanie was shown an ethnic Barbie, she pointed out to me that ethnic Barbie is not a true Barbie but a friend.

> Stephanie: That looks like Barbie's friend.
>
> Janet: This looks like Barbie's friend? Why?
>
> Stephanie: Because she has the black hair and she has earrings … she's black.

Stephanie had identified that the ethnic version of Barbie was not a real Barbie. Stephanie's assessment of the racial disparity between Barbie and ethnic Barbie is reminiscent of the foundational doll test of Clark and Clark (1947) over seventy years ago. The symbolic value of black Barbie for Stephanie was lower than for white Barbie; black Barbie was not viewed as a substitute for white Barbie and will always be the other. As Carolina Acosta-Alzuru and Peggy Kreshel established in 2002, the dominant group values that are imprinted on public consciousness can be seen in these specific notions about family, race, gender, and class, not just in toys, but in other genres of popular culture that may be interpreted as holding social value. An example of how social class stratification is enacted through doll culture was portrayed in an article published in England's *The Daily Telegraph* in 2010. Heidi Blake criticized Walmart for selling black Barbie dolls at half the price of white Barbies. The article highlighted how disparaging tropes are circulated in advertisements and popular culture. Consumers, including girls and young women, of course, internalize these myths as truths.

Rather than accept a bland understanding of black culture, Jennifer, like the other participants, carved a niche for herself by repurposing doll play to incorporate aspects of blackness such as braiding the hair of their white dolls. These then become avatars for an aesthetic that reflected black identity. Although Hains (2012) notes in her survey that the Bratz dolls were sexualized, her girl participants did not focus on this. My findings with the young people in Toronto were similar. In my study, they were enamored with the visible metrics of racialized identity, particularly skin color and hair. Tracy, aged 12, liked the multicultural flavors of Bratz dolls because of their diversity and inclusivity. She used her Bratz dolls for role playing games in her aspirations to be a teacher or hairstylist.

> Tracy: Sometimes my friend comes over and we play with them like school or stuff like hairstylist, or something like that.
>
> Janet: When you play school with your dolls, what do you do?
>
> Tracy: We usually … pretend to move the dolls and pretend to make them say stuff.
>
> Janet: So you are the teacher and they are the students?
>
> Tracy: Yes.

Both Sabrina and Jennifer related to their ethnic Barbie dolls in a nonsexualized way.

> Janet: When you were playing with Barbie, did you want to look like Barbie?
>
> Sabrina: The black Barbie, yes.
>
> Janet: What was different about black Barbie?
>
> Sabrina: She had a different smile and was brighter, and I liked her cheeks better. Her hair was still the same as Barbie but matched her better.

In playing with her black Barbie, Sabrina purposely described black Barbie with positive characteristics, while Jennifer made a point of detailing activities in which her black Barbie did not partake.

> Jennifer: I saw a cool teenage black girl as her, but she was smarter for some reason, like she wasn't like BET[2] like shaking-her-booty kinda girl.

Jennifer acknowledges the dominant sexualized narrative of the booty-shaking black woman in popular culture, especially hip-hop culture, which suggests limited intelligence. She was quick to say her Barbie was a less visible but a "cool" and "smart" young black girl. By stressing who her doll was not, Jennifer showed how young girls like her see limited

Illustration 8.2 • Sabrina with her American Girl Doll. Photo credit Janet Seow.

images and depictions of black womanhood in North America. This is a contextual dilemma that ethnic girls face every day in being typecast as sexual objects yet rejecting that particular narrative. The girls challenged these stereotypes by repurposing their dolls, be they Barbie or Bratz, through the narratives they created about them. Jennifer's understanding of her positionality—the blockades and stereotypes she will have to fight—placed her in a paradoxical position. She envisioned hardship in life as a visible minority and challenged this subordinate position by rejecting racial identifications. Jennifer's outlook could be interpreted as one that assumes a race-neutral persona which will, we hope, ease the constraints of blackness. She sees herself excelling within an imagined setting that is racially tolerant and non-confrontational. Sabrina, however, demonstrated awareness of the social barriers she may encounter and used doll play to envision attending university and having a successful life.

> Sabrina: It was just like when I'm like bored or like when I feel sad, I just played with them and say like I want my life to be like this when I'm in high school or when I'm in university and all that stuff.

Sabrina used doll play in a positive way to plan for the future she wants to have. Whether or not she is aware that having a university education is a significant factor in mitigation of the barriers that exist for racialized people is unclear.

Scarcity of Ethnic Dolls

The popularity of Bratz dolls and Jennifer's preference for My Scene dolls speaks to the importance of diversity to participation in a racially diverse and complicated world (Hains 2012). This is why 12-year-old Tracy prefers Bratz dolls.

> Janet: Do you play with Barbie dolls?
>
> Tracy: No, not really
>
> Janet: Why?
>
> Tracy: They don't have a lot of black Barbie dolls and they don't really have other cultured dolls, so usually I play with the Bratz dolls because they have different colors and different cultures.

Tracy is critical of how multiculturalism is lacking in doll culture in her acknowledgment of the exclusion of diasporic groups from the broader texts of society which, ironically, is reflected in which dolls are available. For many of these young girls, multiculturalism accords migrant groups an uneven insider/outsider status without a true sense of belonging or of being Canadian. In order to overcome these barriers, black girls are forced to navigate two worlds because they see a limited reflection of themselves in children's material culture. Without a reference, they are left to create their own, which they do through doll play. The available black dolls are American; their narratives are not Caribbean. Each American Girl doll, for instance, is introduced with a story about her background. For example, Addy is a runaway slave. In fact, the areas of focus in black doll research—aesthetic, historic, narrative—have tended to be about American slave trade originals (Bernstein 2011; Martin 2014; Thomas 2007; Wilkinson 1987). I am not aware of any available doll that includes a narrative of any Afro-Caribbean experience with its inclusivity and cosmopolitanism. This means that the acute racism of American black doll culture is not generally reflective of the Toronto Afro-Caribbean experience. Awareness of what Homi

Bhabha (1990) refers to as the hybridity of Caribbean culture is lacking in children's material culture in Canada in spite of a strong multicultural discourse. Rather than the strict confines of black or white dolls, Tracy appreciates the nuanced and complex racial and gendered cosmopolitanism of the Bratz culture which matches multicultural Toronto. The complexity of race, class, and gender found in Bratz dolls is also appealing to 10-year-old Mariah who embraces Bratz as an alternative to the limited supply of black dolls.

> Janet: Do you see black dolls often in the stores?
>
> Mariah: No, not often in the stores, but if you see one, then usually there's only one.
>
> Janet: Do you think there should be more?
>
> Mariah: Yes, definitely.
>
> Janet: Why?
>
> Mariah: Because I just think it's not fair that … other cultures have lots of dolls and we don't.

From Mariah's comments, one must surely infer that some negative effect is taking place in the psyche of black girls. The scarcity of ethnic dolls sends a distinct message to black girls that they are not important or visible to those in positions of power. In addition to this, the limited availability or absence of ethnic dolls in positions of prominence in stores trains white girls to view racialized girls as inferior. When my participating girls did find black dolls, many of them were not authentic in their physical representation, as Mariah explained.

> Janet: Do you think having black dolls helps black girls?
>
> Mariah: Yes.
>
> Janet: In what way?
>
> Mariah: It helps them to see themselves represented with all the other races.
>
> Janet: Do you think the black dolls that are available look like black children?
>
> Mariah: Certain ones do … depending on the type of doll that it is. Sometimes it's not like an actual black person.
>
> Janet: What about the black doll is unlike a black person?
>
> Mariah: For me … like the most obvious for me, is the hair. Usually black people don't have the type of hair that they show on dolls.

Mariah's comments show her awareness that it is seen to be more important to make an authentic doll representation of a white girl than of a black one. These girls' and young women's recognition of themselves as outsiders is most evident when girls play with the expensive and exclusive American Girl dolls that offer a patriarchal, adult-centered view of girls while at the same time purporting to address the needs of a multicultural society (duCille 1996). Only a few ethnic identities are available in the American Girl doll line, and these remain grounded in the dominant group's imagination that associates particular physical and social characteristics with those thought of as other. Acosta-Alzuru and Kreshel (2002) offer a robust example of racial stratification in two dolls from the American Doll collection. In her personal narrative, the Swedish immigrant doll, Kristen, can quickly assimilate and blend into her environment, but Josefina, a Mexican doll, remains deeply entrenched in her ethnic roots in her narrative. These contrasting narratives highlight a serious disparity in the potential of the European immigrant represented by the European doll Kristen, compared to the Mexican immigrant as represented by the Mexican doll Josefina.

Like Disney and Mattel, American Girl has significant reach into the homes, lives, and psyche of girls. Similar to their doll play with Barbie and Bratz, their American Girl doll play speaks to black girls' understanding of positionality and self-identity in a biased world. An example of this is reflected in Sabrina's comments on owning an American Girl doll.

> Sabrina: I do have my favorite doll … She is like an American Girl doll … I named her Emma … I like her eyes and her hair … she has blonde hair, blondish, brownish, it looks red, but it's blonde and she has blue eyes and rosy cheeks.
>
> Janet: What is special about Emma?
>
> Sabrina: Well, it's mostly, I think because of the value, because she was $145, so just the value of her and … I never had a doll like this … I wanted an American Girl doll for a long time, but I didn't want my mom to be paying for it because it's a lot of money. I bought it with my own money, so if I wreck it, I have nothing to feel bad for because I didn't waste my mom's money for no reason … So, since I bought it with my own money, it makes me feel more proud that I bought it, but the next doll I'm gonna get is gonna look like me, because the one that I was gonna to get that looked like me, they didn't have any more.

Janet: You wanted a black doll?

Sabrina: Sort of, but it was either Emma, or the look-alike doll, but then I'm like okay, how about I get my first doll not to look like me, but just like a normal person, and then my next doll would be a black doll and she would have the curly hair.

Sabrina's reflection on saving to buy her American Girl Emma doll suggests that the economic investment was a completely self-directed purchase and an important moment in consumption agency for a 12-year-old. In this purchase, we see racialized belonging and ideas of beauty prioritized through doll ownership, and thus "normal person" Emma was her first choice. Choosing Emma reflects the alienation of being black and an acute understanding of blackness in society. A black American Girl doll is not as valuable as Emma. The identity of blackness is not preferred. This aversion informs Sabrina's choices and perception about black identity. We see here the genesis of decisions not only in dolls, but life choices such as jobs, clothes, and residences (see Hains 2012; Wilkinson 1987). As a huge financial decision, Sabrina's money is on Emma, the gold standard of children's play and culture. She is able to experience this standard vicariously through the doll. This is a doll Sabrina could confidently bring to school, a doll with white features and hair she could fuss over, and this would guarantee that she was not excluded in her choices but, instead, would be praised in a multicultural space where white is still the aspirational standard.

Unlike Jennifer who could articulate that her doll was not the dominant, sexualized black woman on television, Sabrina's ownership of Emma addresses the trickiness of black identity politics, especially for girls who do not yet have the vocabulary and skills to challenge the racial hierarchies of neoliberal consumption and playground racism. Sabrina's strategy of planning her future purchase of a curly-haired, black American Girl doll appears to be one of building confidence and the skills needed to showcase her black doll and her own blackness. I want to understand Sabrina's purchase of the Emma doll not as a rejection of her blackness, but as a girl who is doing self-work and learning to build skills to face a racist world.

Analysis

The earlier historical overview in this article shows how the past leaves black children in a continuous state of otherness, both explicit and implicit. Responses from the Toronto respondents showcase how this otherness is felt in contemporary Canadian society. Young women and girls demonstrate they are social actors and agents of change in their own lives as they negotiate a place for themselves in a society that renders them either invisible or highly sexualized. They change narratives, build skills, and seek alternatives in a racially hierarchal space and, through doll play, black girls learn to become discerning consumers of a doll culture coded with values of the dominant patriarchal white society. Repurposing doll play to reflect enriched narratives such as career aspirations and race pride indicate their ability to subversively reject the dominant group's inscribed identities and social characteristics. As an example, Sabrina, Tracey, and Mariah transform their white dolls with Afrocentric styles such as braids. They describe their actions during doll play.

> Sabrina: I used to do their hair, use my hair products, then braid their hair and everything.
>
> Tracy: Sometimes they have long hair … they are fun to play with. You could do their hair easy.
>
> Mariah: I just usually do whatever with their hair. I don't usually play games with them … I like to do their hair.

For young black girls, hair texture is one of the most distinguishing physical features of being black females. Caring for their hair, particularly for young girls, is a time consuming and important ritual. This is the locus of intergenerational teachings and support. Omitting or downplaying this feature on black dolls is crucial but, as Chin (1999) and Hains (2012) have suggested, by changing their dolls' hair styles, the girls show agency in coming to terms with their exclusion by imprinting their identity as black girls on their white dolls in order to create meaning and give purpose to their existence. In addition to practicing doing hair, white-haired Barbie becomes a discursive space in which young black girls can invent and formulate oppositional interpretations of their ascribed identities, interests, and needs. Boundary crossing is manifested when racialized children move seamlessly between black and white cultures. The physical transformation of white dolls through their having braids becomes an effective way to introduce black culture subversively into white spaces.

The examination of ethnic doll culture and doll play is a way to understand race and representations of blackness in the girlhoods of Afro-Caribbean youth in Toronto and the interdependency between past and present. Doll play mimics the larger social relationships and ideological narratives that help black girls understand their subordinate roles.

Bratz dolls are a diverse set of multicultural dolls which are perceived as problematic by various cultural critics because of their sexually suggestive representations (American Psychologists Association 2007; Whitney 2012), yet young people were able to look beyond perceived limitations of Bratz dolls and they found ways to use their imagination and creativity. Barbie has been criticized for her unrealistic form as an unattainable ideal. Yet Barbie's iconic status and power cannot be denied. She has been the mainstay of girls for approximately 60 years and remains a staple in every household with girls three years of age and up (Graff et al. 2012). In her interview, Jennifer describes using Barbie as a fashion muse and an imagined positive role model.

> Jennifer: I look at how pretty my Barbie dress and sometimes it would be like look at all these clothes that Barbie gets to have. This is a legitimate fantasy that I had. I wished there was a machine that could enlarge Barbie doll's clothes so that I could wear them and then a machine that can make me smaller if I wanted to go to Barbie doll size. Like that was basically what I used my Barbie dolls for. It wasn't like oh, I wish my face looked like her, or I wish my body looked like her. It's just I wish I could wear the clothes she could.

Jennifer confirms aspects of Jacqueline Reid-Walsh and Claudia Mitchell's (2009) Canadian research findings that highlight the popularity of the Barbie brand and its impact on the psyche of Canadian girlhood. Their thoughtful analysis delves into the personal meanings attached to dolls through their everyday use by girls as playthings. Their findings reveal that girls have unique relationships with their dolls that are coded with social norms and mores which ultimately transform the meaning of dolls from commodities, or objects, to material. Reid-Walsh and Mitchell report girls in Canada, for example, as viewing Barbie's appearance as empowering because she shows the possibilities of work outside the domestic setting. Barbie play inspires young people to challenge gender-specific roles and is credited with influencing their career choices.

The doll play process starts at an early age for racialized young girls and, with repeated reinforcements, racial myths become values and beliefs in the psyche of both black and white children, perhaps particularly girls. For Jennifer, embracing the image of Barbie may serve to construct and reconstruct her self-esteem and identity. She uses the image of Barbie as an inspiration as well as a form of resistance by repurposing the subordinate role of black Barbie into that of a leader, a positive affirmation of blackness that counteracts racism, sexism, and social class differentiation.

In addition to its popularity, the American Girl dolls' strengths are anatomical correctness and flexibility for customization. American Girl doll accessories provide access to girls' play culture in which imaginative play provides opportunities for girls to see themselves as unique individuals. Sabrina appreciates the beauty and difference in her white Emma doll as well as her own uniqueness as a black girl. Her plan to purchase a black lookalike doll suggests her coming to terms with her blackness as an essential factor in her identity formation.

Conclusion

Doll play is an important route to understanding girls' culture and identity formation because not only is it an expression of their play culture, it is also a fun-filled activity that allows imagination and creativity to flourish. Girls' and young women's self-esteem and confidence are increased when they see themselves in an object of pleasure like a beloved doll. Older girls like Jennifer develop empowering aspects of black identity through doll play. Jennifer does this by creating narratives that construct her doll as smart and successful. But Sabrina, who is younger, does not yet have this confidence. Her financial sacrifice for an American Girl doll justifies only the safe Emma who is white, beautiful, and publicly acceptable. I believe she unconsciously uses her future doll purchase as a target to meet in order to develop skills to navigate a racially unequal world.

My qualitative survey highlights how further research on black girls and their doll cultures is warranted, particularly in a multicultural city like Toronto where race is seldom a simple issue of black and white, but is, rather, embedded in diasporic realities.

Janet Rosemarie Seow (ORCID: https://orcid.org/0000-0002-9213-6946) is a doctoral candidate in the department of Humanities and a research associate at the Centre for Research on Latin America and the Caribbean at York University in Toronto, Ontario, Canada. Her research interests include participatory research with Afro-Canadian children and youth and their engagement with material culture; Global cultures of children and youth; young adult literature; Indigenous literature; Afrofuturism literature; critical theory; critical race theory; gender studies; pedagogy of kindness; social justice pedagogy; and anti-racist pedagogy.

Acknowledgments

I thank the parents and children for their consent and, in particular, the girls and young women who so thoughtfully participated in the study that formed the basis of this research.

Notes

1. My Scene dolls were fashion dolls created by Mattel in 2002.
2. Black Entertainment Television (BET) models are scantily dressed in music videos.

References

Acosta-Alzuru, Carolina, and Peggy J. Kreshel. 2002. "I'm an American Girl … Whatever that Means: Girl Consuming Pleasant Company's American Girl Identity." *Journal of Communication* 52 (1): 139–161. doi: 10.1111/j.1460-2466.2002.t602536.x

Alderson, Priscilla, and Virginia Morrow. 2011. *The Ethics of Research with Children and Young People: A Practical Handbook.* London: SAGE.

American Psychological Association. 2007. Report of the APA Task Force on the Sexualization of Girls. http://www/apa.org/pi/women/programs/girls/report.aspx (accessed 30 July 2016).

Bernstein, Robin. 2011. *Racial Innocence: Performing American Childhood from Slavery to Civil Rights.* New York: New York University Press.

Blake, Heidi. 2010. "Walmart Under Fire for Selling Black Barbies at Half Price of White Dolls." *The Daily Telegraph,* 11 March.

Bhabha, Homi.1990. "The Third Space." In *Identity: Community, Culture, Difference,* ed. Jonathan Rutherford, 207–221. London: Lawrence & Wishart.

Bushin, Naomi. 2007. "Interviewing with Children in their Homes: Putting Ethical Principles into Practice and Developing Flexible Techniques." *Children's Geographies* 5 (3): 235–251. doi: 10.1080/14733280701445796

Chakraborty, Kabita. 2009. "The Good Muslim Girl: Conducting Qualitative Participatory Research to Understand the Lives of Young Muslim Women in the Bustees of Kolkata." *Children's Geographies* 7 (4): 421–434. doi:10.1080/14733280903234485

Chin, Elizabeth. 1999. "Ethnically Correct Dolls: Toying with the Race Industry." *American Anthropologist* 101 (2): 305–321. doi: 10.1525/aa.1999.101.2.305

Clark, Kenneth, and Mamie Clark. 1947. "Racial Identification and Preference in Negro Children." In *Readings in Social Psychology*, ed. T. M. Newcomb and E. L. Hartley, 169–178. New York: Holt.

duCille, Ann. 1994. "Dyes and Dolls: Multicultural Barbie and the Merchandizing of Difference." *Difference: A Journal of Feminist Cultural Studies* 6 (1): 47–68.

duCille, Ann.1996. *Skin Trade*. Cambridge, MA: Harvard University Press.

Ennew, Judith. 2009. *The Right to Be Properly Researched: How to Do Rightsbased, Scientific Research with Children*. Bangkok: Black on White Publications.

Graff, Kaitlin, Sarah K. Murnen, and Linda Smolak. 2012. "Too Sexualized to be Taken Seriously? Perceptions of a Girl in Childlike vs. Sexualizing Clothing." *Sex Roles* 66: 764–775. doi: 10.1007/s11199-012-0145-3

Hains, Rebecca C. 2012. "An Afternoon of Productive Play with Problematic Dolls: The Importance of Foregrounding Children's Voices in Research." *Girlhood Studies: An Interdisciplinary Journal* 5 (1): 121–140. doi:10.3167/ghs.2012.050108

James, Allison. 2007. "Giving Voice to Children's Voices: Practices and Problems, Pitfalls and Potentials." *American Anthropologist* 109 (2): 261–272. doi: 10./525/aa.2007.109.2.261

Martin, Anthony. 2014 "Toys with Professions: Racialized Black Dolls, 1850–1940." *Journal of African Diaspora Archaeology and Heritage* 3 (2): 137–158. doi.org/10.1179/21619441142.00000000016

Reid-Walsh, Jaqueline, and Claudia Mitchell. 2009 "Mapping a Canadian Girlhood Historically Through Dolls and Dolls-Play." In *Depicting Canada's Children*, ed. Loren Lerner, 109–132. Waterloo: Wilfred Laurier University Press.

Rogers, Mary F. 1999. *Barbie Culture*. Thousand Oaks, CA: SAGE.

Schwarz, Maureen Trudelle. 2005. "Native American Barbie: The Marketing of Euro American Desires." *American Studies* 46 (3/4): 295–326.

Thomas, Sabrina Lynette. 2007. "Sara Lee: The Rise and Fall of the Ultimate Negro Doll." *Transforming Anthropology* 15 (1): 30– 49. doi: tran.2007.15.1.38

Whitney, Jennifer Dawn. 2012. "Some Assembly Required: Black Barbie and the Fabrication of Nicki Minaj." *Girlhood Studies: An Interdisciplinary Journal* 5 (1): 141–159. doi:10.3167/ghs.2012.050109

Wilkinson, Doris Yvonne. 1974. "Racial Socialization through Children's Toys: A Sociohistorical Examination." *Journal of Black Studies* 5 (1): 96–109.

Wilkinson, Doris Yvonne. 1987. "The Doll Exhibit: A Psycho-Cultural Analysis of Black Female Role Stereotypes." *The Journal of Popular Culture* 21 (2):19–30. doi: 10.1111/j.0022-3840.1987.2102-19.x

Index

❧